P9-ARY-114

**New Directions for
Higher Education**

Betsy O. Barefoot
Jillian L. Kinzie
Co-editors

Mentoring as Transformative Practice: Supporting Student and Faculty Diversity

Caroline S. Turner

EDITOR

Number 171 • Fall 2015
Jossey-Bass
San Francisco

MENTORING AS TRANSFORMATIVE PRACTICE: SUPPORTING STUDENT AND
FACULTY DIVERSITY
Caroline S. Turner
New Directions for Higher Education, no. 171
Betsy O. Barefoot and Jillian L. Kinzie, Co-editors

Microfilm copies of issues and articles are available in 16mm and 35mm,
as well as microfiche in 105mm, through University Microfilms Inc., 300
North Zeeb Road, Ann Arbor, MI 48106-1346.

NEW DIRECTIONS FOR HIGHER EDUCATION (ISSN 0271-0560, electronic ISSN
1536-0741) is part of The Jossey-Bass Higher and Adult Education Series and is published quarterly by Wiley Subscription Services, Inc., A
Wiley Company, at Jossey-Bass, One Montgomery Street, Suite 1200, San
Francisco, CA 94104-4594. Periodicals Postage Paid at San Francisco,
California, and at additional mailing offices. POSTMASTER: Send address
changes to New Directions for Higher Education, Jossey-Bass, One Montgomery Street, Suite 1200, San Francisco, CA 94104-4594.

New Directions for Higher Education is indexed in Current Index to Journals in Education (ERIC); Higher Education Abstracts.

Individual subscription rate (in USD): $89 per year US/Can/Mex, $113
rest of world; institutional subscription rate: $335 US, $375 Can/Mex,
$409 rest of world. Single copy rate: $29. Electronic only–all re-
gions: $89 individual, $335 institutional; Print & Electronic–US:
$98 individual, $402 institutional; Print & Electronic–Canada/Mexico:
$98 individual, $442 institutional; Print & Electronic–Rest of World:
$122 individual, $476 institutional.

Editorial correspondence should be sent to the Co-editor, Betsy O.
Barefoot, Gardner Institute, Box 72, Brevard, NC 28712.

Cover design: Wiley
Cover Images: © Lava 4 images | Shutterstock

www.josseybass.com

Contents

EDITOR'S NOTES

Research on diverse students and faculty in academe invariably identifies mentoring as critical to their persistence and advancement (Turner & González, 2014; Turner, González, & Wood, 2008). Definitions of mentoring vary in concept and practice due to its complex and highly individualized nature. Blackwell's (1989) definition was used to begin discussions for this special issue. Blackwell defines mentorship as a process in which a person of superior rank, achievement, and prestige counsels, instructs, and guides the intellectual development of his or her mentee(s). This process can also guide the protégé's social and career development. In essence, the mentorship relationship is one that is built on trust and can result in lifelong, bidirectional benefits for both the mentor and the protégé. Delving into the nuances of the mentoring relationship, researchers conclude, "The goal of mentoring is not simply to teach the system, but also to change the system so that it becomes more flexible and responsive to the needs and pathways of its members—mentors and protégés" (Bernstein, Jacobson, & Russo, 2010, p. 58).

In *Mentoring as Transformative Practice: Supporting Student and Faculty Diversity*, several education scholars, recognized for their contributions as mentors, provide the reader with chapters describing their successes. They articulate the emergence of successful interpersonal mentoring relationships and mentoring programs. Chapters 1 through 5 provide insights into mentor–protégé relationships for men and women of color, within and across race and gender. They illustrate the importance of investing in the relationship-building process, of mentoring practices as social justice work, and of creating affirming learning environments. Chapters 6 and 7 describe the development of online and in-person mentoring programs that support resiliency, self-efficacy, and the expansion of supportive networks for women and minorities in the fields of science, technology, engineering, and mathematics (STEM). Chapters 8 through 10 delineate research-based programs targeted to promote college success for Latino males, to explicate a Latina faculty peer mentoring program based on a pedagogy for equity, and to present an interdisciplinary academic writing program based on enacting feminist alliance principles. In sum, the authors not only provide

NEW DIRECTIONS FOR HIGHER EDUCATION, no. 171, Fall 2015 © 2015 Wiley Periodicals, Inc.
Published online in Wiley Online Library (wileyonlinelibrary.com) • DOI: 10.1002/he.20136

guiding principles underlying successful mentorships, interpersonally and programmatically, but also point to the potential of mentoring, in the many forms presented here, to profoundly transform higher education to better serve the needs of all its members.

Caroline S. Turner
Editor

References

Bernstein, B. L., Jacobson, R., & Russo, N. F. (2010). Mentoring women in context: Focus on science, technology, engineering, and mathematics fields. In C. A. Rayburn, F. L. Denmark, M. E. Reuder, & A. M. Austria (Eds.), *The Praeger handbook for women mentors: Transcending barriers of stereotype, race, and ethnicity* (pp. 43–64). Westport, CT: Praeger.

Blackwell, J. E. (1989). Mentoring: An action strategy for increasing minority faculty. *Academe, 75*(5), 8–14.

Turner, C. S. V., & González, J. C. (Eds.). (2014). *Modeling mentoring across race/ethnicity and gender: Practices to cultivate the next generation of diverse faculty.* Sterling, VA: Stylus.

Turner, C. S. V., González, J. C., & Wood, J. L. (2008). Faculty of color in academe: What 20 years of literature tells us. *Journal of Diversity in Higher Education, 1*(3), 139–168.

CAROLINE S. TURNER *is professor and graduate coordinator for the Doctorate in Educational Leadership Program at California State University, Sacramento, and is Arizona State University Lincoln professor emerita of higher education and ethics.*

1

Informed by the literature and professional practice, this chapter examines the unique mentoring challenges facing women and underrepresented minorities in higher education. Findings indicate that traditional mentoring approaches fall short in fully supporting the needs of underrepresented populations in higher education.

Mentoring Outside the Line: The Importance of Authenticity, Transparency, and Vulnerability in Effective Mentoring Relationships

Sharon Fries-Britt, Jeanette Snider

As increasing numbers of women and underrepresented minorities (URMs) gain access to colleges and universities (American Council on Education, 2011), they are likely to encounter academic and social barriers to their success and retention (Hurtado & Guillermo-Wann, 2013; Swail, Redd, & Perna, 2003). Connections to campus agents like faculty and staff are the strongest predictors of success among college students in general (Pascarella & Terenzini, 2005), and evidence suggests that faculty also play a critical role in the success of racial and ethnic minority students (Davis, 2010; Museus, Palmer, Davis, & Maramba, 2011; Pascarella, 1980; Patton & Harper, 2003; Waldeck, Orrego, Plax, & Kearney, 1997). The importance of having mentors for women and URM students is well documented (Davis, 2010; Fries-Britt & Turner Kelly, 2005; Grant, 2012; Pascarella, 1980; Patton & Harper, 2003; Turner, 2002). At predominantly White institutions (PWIs), URMs can encounter feelings of isolation and uncertainty about their capabilities in their respective fields of study. Mentoring can be an effective strategy to combat many of these challenges.

This chapter examines important aspects of mentoring that impact women and URMs in higher education. This work is shaped in two important ways. First, we turn to the mentoring literature as it pertains to women and URMs in higher education. From the literature we highlight several key factors impacting mentoring for women and underrepresented populations. Second, we turn to our own professional experiences as mentees and mentors. We each present a brief narrative in which we share key

NEW DIRECTIONS FOR HIGHER EDUCATION, no. 171, Fall 2015 © 2015 Wiley Periodicals, Inc.
Published online in Wiley Online Library (wileyonlinelibrary.com) • DOI: 10.1002/he.20137

components of our own mentoring experiences and philosophy. As Black women, our racial identities have been important factors in our own experiences in higher education and thus add meaning to how we understand the mentoring process. We conclude this work by offering recommendations that reflect a set of guiding principles to cultivate underrepresented students' authentic professional development in higher education.

Literature on Mentoring URMs and Women

In a review of the literature on mentoring, Museus and associates (2011), in an Association for the Study of Higher Education (ASHE) report, suggest that underrepresented minorities across institutional types found that "faculty and other institutional agents (advisors, counselors, and student affairs staff) who shared common ground with students humanized the educational experience, provided holistic support, and were proactive in serving minority students had a positive influence on those participants' success" (p. 72). These relationships have the potential of removing feelings of isolation that many undergraduate and graduate students, as well as faculty of color, experience at PWIs. In a recent study, Strayhorn's (2010) participants described faculty as mentors and "cultural navigators" throughout the educational and professional process. In this chapter, we examine three key themes addressed in the mentorship literature: (1) academic and/or psychosocial needs of students, (2) role modeling, and (3) same versus cross race and gender mentor relationships.

Academic Versus Psychosocial.   Kram's (1988) seminal work focuses on two dimensions of mentorship: academic and psychosocial development. Academic development refers to the socialization of graduate students and junior faculty into their specific fields. Mentoring is particularly important at the graduate level as students attempt to navigate their academic process. Connecting with faculty for research opportunities, gaining publication experience, and presenting at national conferences are critical at the graduate level. Positive relationships between faculty and students based on trust, integrity, opportunity, and understanding have a critical impact on student persistence (Patton & Harper, 2003).

While academic development addresses professional opportunities, the psychosocial supports attempt to address the protégés' personal well-being and confidence in their academic abilities and in personal identity. Black women provide a unique style of mentorship focusing on the holistic development of future scholars. African American women understand the complex intersectionality of race and gender in higher education that is unique to their population (Grant, 2012). Fries-Britt and Turner Kelly's (2005) work demonstrated this complexity well. Over the course of a decade, they established a level of connection that allowed them to rely on one another during critical times in their academic careers. What started as a faculty mentor and graduate student relationship emerged into a deeper

NEW DIRECTIONS FOR HIGHER EDUCATION • DOI: 10.1002/he

connection. In their work, Fries-Britt and Turner Kelly write about the risks they each took in their relationship to move outside of the formal roles into a more reciprocal relationship that allowed for more depth and growth in their relationship over time.

Role Modeling.   It is important that URMs and women have access to colleagues who can help them negotiate their experiences in the academy. Research demonstrates that Black faculty model success for students of color (Banks, 1984; Fries-Britt & Turner Kelly, 2005; Griffin, 2012; Plata, 1996). Griffin (2012) found that faculty view themselves in a broader context, describing themselves as a link in a "longer chain of relationships" (p. 45). Black faculty learned how to mentor by mimicking the positive characteristics of their mentors. Not only is mentoring important to improve the academic and social experiences of students of color at PWIs, but Griffin found that these critical relationships shape mentoring behaviors for future generations. Role modeling is critically important in the mentoring process for minorities. "By their very existence, mentors provide proof that the journey can be made" (Daloz, 1999, p. 207). Although the academy can be harsh and can present barriers, mentors provide a roadmap for their students or junior-level faculty that can sustain them in the field and offer lasting benefits.

Same and Cross Race/Gender.   Students of color seek out faculty of color as mentors to gain "support, guidance, and mentorship, perceiving those professors as having a unique understanding of their experiences" (Griffin, 2012, p. 32). If available, African American doctoral students prefer same-race mentors (Patton, 2009; Tillman, 2001). Traditionally, mentor relationships have been defined through a Eurocentric lens, which is typically a short-term and more academically focused experience (Fries-Britt & Griffin, 2007; Waldeck et al., 1997). For African American students and faculty, their relationship is reciprocal and both parties benefit from these close relationships (Fries-Britt & Turner Kelly, 2005).

Researchers have found that within some same-race interactions, faculty members can inspire students by sharing their own struggles and empathizing with their fears (Fries-Britt & Turner Kelly, 2005; Fries-Britt, Younger, & Hall, 2010). Same-race/gender faculty can relate to feelings of marginality that students may be experiencing at a PWI (Davis, 2010). While the literature states that African American doctoral students prefer same-race mentors, given the low number of Black doctoral students and subsequently low numbers of faculty of color, these pairs are unlikely to be found in their own department, if at all (Adams, 1992; Fries-Britt et al., 2010).

The low number of minority faculty available to mentor students in the academy only increases the importance of cross-race mentorship (Davis, 2007). Students seek mentors with a commitment to foster their academic success (Patton, 2009). Consequently, the racial/ethnic makeup of the faculty mentor is not a major factor in terms of support (Adams,

1992; Fries-Britt et al., 2010; Ong, Wright, Espinosa, & Orfield, 2011). Most racial/ethnic minority undergraduate and graduate students have mentors who are male and White (Ong et al., 2011). The most important criteria for choosing a mentor should be the amount of time available and interest in accepting new protégés with the intention of providing the proper guidance, support, and encouragement (Adams, 1992, p. 3). As long as nonminority faculty members are culturally aware and open to working with diverse populations, these relationships can be fruitful (Fries-Britt, 1998; Patton & Harper, 2003).

Typically, White faculty members serve primarily as academic advisors and less as personal mentors for students of color. In some cases, African American students feel as though they cannot be vulnerable with cross-race mentors because they will be perceived as weak (Patton & Harper, 2003). Although challenging, cross-race mentor relationships are common and can provide students with the information and support they need to persist. Patton (2009) submits that if students are engaged in cross-race mentorships and are *not* being supported emotionally, these students can find alternative outlets, such as friends and family, to supplement the lack of nurturing from their professors. Mentoring is critical at all levels of development, and research affirms the need for these relationships at every stage in the professional career of URMs and women.

Reflections From Practice

As coauthors we both work extensively with diverse communities of students on our campus and nationally in the field of higher education. Our own experiences reflect many of the findings in the literature about the importance of same-race, and same-gender, mentors and role models in higher education (Adams, 1992; Banks, 1984; Daloz, 1999; Davis, 2007; Fries-Britt & Turner Kelly, 2005; Fries-Britt et al., 2010; Griffin, 2012; Ong et al., 2011; Patton, 2009; Patton & Harper, 2003; Plata, 1996; Tillman, 2001). We believe that our own experiences in the academy, combined with the literature, offer important insights and lessons for practice. We turn next to our personal narratives and mentoring philosophy, and then offer suggestions for practice.

Jeanette.   I discovered the powerful impact that mentors could have on the success of students on a personal level when I enrolled at a competitive PWI. As I contemplated transferring to another institution, potentially exposing myself to transfer shock (Laanan, 2001) and even greater episodes of isolation, I experienced the invaluable benefits of mentor/mentee relationships. Three administrators at my undergraduate institution took an interest in my life. Little did they know that their willingness to mentor me would lead to my successful undergraduate experience and later would directly influence my career goals. As a higher education professional, I try to embody similar traits as my mentors had (Griffin, 2012). Through my own personal experiences as a protégé and my lived experience as a mentor to similarly gifted minority students, I have learned how to reach my students and maintain a long-lasting relationship well after they graduate. Successful characteristics that lead to impactful mentoring behavior include being genuine in my interactions, exhibiting transparency, and being open to reciprocity. Students can sense authenticity. I joined this profession because I genuinely care about the success of students. I approach them with tough love and a sincere heart. I celebrate their successes and encourage them to push harder when I see they are not maximizing their potential.

The final two elements work together: transparency and reciprocity. Although I am in the early stages of my career, I have made mistakes and encountered numerous barriers in the academy. I hope my transparency will result in students' ability to (1) relate to my experiences (role modeling), (2) feel comfortable sharing their experiences, and (3) avoid some of my pitfalls in the future. My willingness to share my experiences results in my students' willingness to be more transparent with their experiences. Even more important, they are comfortable providing me with feedback about my mentoring. I struggle with many of the same insecurities and life challenges as my students. At times, my mentees sustain and encourage me. Relationships are nothing if they are not reciprocal. This is one of the many elements of the mentorship process that has been powerful in my journey. By simply coauthoring this article with my mentor, this collaboration is a product of the very same advisory elements that have sustained me in the academy and now contribute to my own mentoring practices.

Sharon.   In 2011, I received the mentoring award from the Association for the Study of Higher Education (ASHE). While I certainly consider myself to be committed to mentoring and intentional about the ways that I interact with students, I was nevertheless deeply moved by this recognition.

How we were mentored matters. Like others, my commitment to mentoring grew as a result of my own experiences with critical adults and professionals in my life. I can point to my parents, aunts, and uncles as well as other family members who played an important role in helping me recognize my talents. Another layer of mentors came as a result of my interactions with effective teachers who affirmed my academic and nonacademic abilities. Although I encountered some negative teachers and can recall incidents that caused me to question my own competence, I was able to use these as motivation to succeed.

A pivotal group of mentors came along in the early part of my professional career. This was a diverse group of individuals by gender, race, religion, and certainly philosophical perspectives. I quickly labeled this group as my core team (e.g., doctoral advisor, senior-level administrators, and several college presidents). In hindsight I now know that they were, in fact, a "dream team" of mentors to have access to. They are straightforward in sharing their perspectives. They talk very directly with me about race and gender and my experiences as an African American woman; however, they never have placed limits on me based on these factors. Rather, they understand that these identities can play a role in my experiences, so they deal with them directly. While they each have unique strengths, what they share in common is their own psychological well-being. At first glance, this may seem like an odd characteristic to identify; however, it is directly connected to their mentoring effectiveness. I believe that effective mentoring requires a degree of personal well-being. Fortunately, my mentors have been able to offer me guidance as secure individuals with a sense of purpose and passion in their own lives. I leave their company feeling inspired and challenged and knowing that I matter. I know that I carry some of what they taught me into my current philosophy of mentoring.

Over time I have consciously developed guiding principles to inform and establish meaningful and authentic relationships with my students. I have learned that it is important to help students cultivate their own lives and not clone my ambitions in them. I strive for transparency in my relationships. Admittedly, this can be a challenge given the complexity of issues that manifest over the course of a student's career, yet it is important to be clear and honest about expectations. I have learned to be okay with vulnerability as a faculty member. I know I don't have all the answers and I encourage my students to ask when they don't understand, and I would like to think that I model this often. Last but certainly not least, I try to be as authentic as I can be in my interactions. This is not always easy, but I try to show up in my professional life in ways that are in alignment with my personal values.

Guiding Principles for Mentoring URMs and Women

As coauthors we are at different stages in our careers; however, we have experienced similar truths about what matters in mentoring. When we consider our own experiences and the literature on mentoring women and URMs, we recognize several consistent themes worth highlighting for practice. We offer these as additional factors to add on to what is already working in mentoring programs and in the personal approaches of faculty. They are offered as guiding principles and not requirements of mentoring, and they reflect increasingly what we see in the literature about the importance of (1) building authentic relationships, (2) transparency and trust, and (3) learning to live with vulnerability.

Build Authentic Mentoring Relationships.   Minority faculty and students seek meaningful relationships that may start from a formal connection; however, over time they develop respect, a strong ethic of care, and sincere value for one another (Griffin, 2012; Patton & Harper, 2003). These deeper levels of appreciation allow the relationship to expand and withstand more significant incidents over time. Building authentic relationships is not an excuse for lack of accountability. In authentic relationships, both faculty and students should feel comfortable expressing concerns and disappointments while developing a strategy for moving forward. Mentoring relationships that seek authenticity will strengthen and not diminish over time (Fries-Britt & Turner Kelly, 2005), especially if both parties understand that authenticity can be maintained when things are going well and when they are not.

Transparency and Trust Are Essential. Transparency and trust are not always easy to establish. It is important for minority faculty, students, and women to have someone they can talk to about their experiences without fear of reprisal (Fries-Britt & Turner Kelly, 2005; Fries-Britt et al., 2010; Patton & Harper, 2003). Even more important, they need someone to talk to who is in their corner who can help them academically as well as psychologically (Davis, 2007; Patton, 2009; Tillman, 2001). Effective mentors seek to establish transparency and trust early in the relationship. One strategy for building both is when mentors model these behaviors (Griffin, 2012). When transparency and trust are in place, the relationship can deepen and gain strength that fortifies the relationship for decades.

Learning to Live With Vulnerability. Anytime a relationship is established between two individuals, a space of vulnerability has been opened. The values and expectations that many minority and women faculty and students bring to the mentoring process suggest that even greater degrees of vulnerability are likely to be experienced. Given that typically academic and psychological needs are being considered in the interactions that minority faculty have with minority students, many potentially challenging topics can surface. As revealed in the literature (Patton & Harper, 2003), minority students often feel like they cannot show their vulnerability for fear that they will be seen as weak. When both minority faculty and students are comfortable allowing vulnerability (Fries-Britt & Turner Kelly, 2005), this moves the relationship to a new level.

When appropriate, senior faculty should model these behaviors and not wait for students and junior faculty to acknowledge what they already know to be true about the challenges in the academy. Before asking students to share their perspectives, faculty should be willing to provide appropriate examples of challenges that they have encountered. We are not recommending that a state of vulnerability be seen as the norm. Rather, we suggest that it not be avoided in instances where discussing critical issues can help students feel affirmed and validated.

Conclusion

Mentoring is a very complex process, and clearly there are different outcomes that can occur between URM students and minority faculty. The factors we identify from the literature and our own experiences may not reflect others' experiences and needs. Nevertheless, we know from research that increasingly the needs of URMs are not easily met by standard mentoring approaches. Faculty must be willing to mentor outside the lines defined by formal relationships. It is important for faculty to be authentic in their interactions with students and to model behaviors that encourage students to share the challenges they are encountering in the academy. When supportive conditions are created within an environment of trust, both faculty and students report very beneficial relationships that grow and develop over time.

References

Adams, H. G. (1992). *Mentoring: An essential factor in the doctoral process for minority students.* Notre Dame, IN: National Consortium for Graduate Degrees for Minorities in Engineering and Science (GEM).

American Council on Education. (2011). *Minorities in higher education: Twenty-fourth status report 2011 supplement.* Washington, DC: Author.

Banks, W. M. (1984). Afro-American scholars in the university. *American Behavioral Scientist, 27*(3), 325–338.

Daloz, L. A. (1999). *Mentor: Guiding the journey of adult learners.* San Francisco, CA: Jossey-Bass.

Davis, D. (2007). Access to academe: The importance of mentoring to Black students. *Negro Educational Review, 58*(3–4), 217–231.

Davis, D. (2010). The academic influence of mentoring upon African American undergraduate aspirants to the professoriate. *Urban Review: Issues and Ideas in Public Education, 42*(2), 143–158.

Fries-Britt, S. (1998). Moving beyond Black achiever isolation: Experiences of gifted Black collegians. *Journal of Higher Education, 69*(5), 556–576.

Fries-Britt, S., & Griffin, K. A. (2007). The Black box: How high-achieving Blacks resist stereotypes about Black Americans. *Journal of College Student Development, 48*(5), 509–524.

Fries-Britt, S., & Turner Kelly, B. (2005). Retaining each other: Narratives of two African American women in the academy. *Urban Review, 37*(3), 221–242.

Fries-Britt, S. L., Younger, T. K., & Hall, W. D. (2010). Lessons from high-achieving students of color in physics. In S. R. Harper & C. B. Newman (Eds.), *New Directions for Institutional Research: No. 148. Students of color in STEM* (pp. 75–83). San Francisco, CA: Jossey-Bass.

Grant, C. M. (2012). Advancing our legacy: A Black feminist perspective on the significance of mentoring for African-American women in educational leadership. *International Journal of Qualitative Studies in Education (QSE), 25*(1), 101–117.

Griffin, K. A. (2012). Learning to mentor: A mixed methods study of the nature and influence of Black professors' socialization into their roles as mentors. *Journal of the Professoriate, 6*(2), 27–58.

Hurtado, S., & Guillermo-Wann, C. (2013, June). *Diverse learning environments: Assessing and creating conditions for student success—Final report to the Ford Foundation.* Los Angeles, CA: Higher Education Research Institute, University of California, Los Angeles.

Kram, K. E. (1988). *Mentoring at work: Developmental relationships in organizational life.* Lanham, MD: University Press of America.

Laanan, F. S. (2001). Transfer student adjustment. In F. S. Laanan (Ed.), *New Directions for Community Colleges: No. 114. Transfer students: Trends and issues* (pp. 5–13). San Francisco, CA: Jossey-Bass.

Museus, S. D., Palmer, R. T., Davis, R. J., & Maramba, D. (2011). *Racial and ethnic minority student success in STEM education* (ASHE Higher Education Report, Vol. 36, No. 6). San Francisco, CA: Jossey-Bass.

Ong, M., Wright, C., Espinosa, L. L., & Orfield, G. (2011). Inside the double bind: A synthesis of empirical research on undergraduate and graduate women of color in science, technology, engineering, and mathematics. *Harvard Educational Review, 81*(2), 172–209.

Pascarella, E. T. (1980). Student-faculty informal contact and college outcomes. *Review of Educational Research, 50*(4), 545–595.

Pascarella, E. T., & Terenzini, P. T. (2005). *How college affects students: A third decade of research* (Vol. 2). San Francisco, CA: Jossey-Bass.

Patton, L. (2009). My sister's keeper: A qualitative examination of mentoring experiences among African American women in graduate and professional schools. *Journal of Higher Education, 80*(5), 510–537.

Patton, L., & Harper, S. (2003). Mentoring relationships among African American women in graduate and professional schools. In M. F. Howard-Hamilton (Ed.), *New Directions for Student Services: No. 104. Meeting the needs of African American women* (pp. 67–78). San Francisco, CA: Jossey-Bass.

Plata, M. (1996, September). Retaining ethnic minority faculty at institutions of higher education. *Journal of Instructional Psychology, 23*, 221–227.

Strayhorn, T. L. (2010, October 27–30). *Social barriers and supports to underrepresented minorities' success in STEM fields.* Paper presented at the 40th ASEE/IEEE Frontiers in Education Conference, Washington, DC.

Swail, W. S., Redd, K. E., & Perna, L. W. (2003). *Retaining minority students in higher education: A framework for success* (ASHE-ERIC Higher Education Report, Vol. 30, No. 2). San Francisco, CA: Jossey-Bass.

Tillman, L. C. (2001). Mentoring African American faculty in predominantly White institutions. *Research in Higher Education, 42*(3), 295–325.

Turner, C. S. V. (2002). Women of color in academe. *Journal of Higher Education, 73*(1), 74–93.

Waldeck, J., Orrego, V., Plax, T., & Kearney, P. (1997). Graduate student/faculty mentoring relationships: Who gets mentored, how it happens, and to what end. *Communication Quarterly, 45*(3), 93–109.

Sharon Fries-Britt is a full professor of higher education at the University of Maryland, College Park, and director of the Higher Education, Student Affairs, and International (HESI) Program.

Jeanette Snider is assistant director for the Office of Undergraduate Programs in the Robert H. Smith School of Business at the University of Maryland. She is also a first-year doctoral student in the Higher Education Program at the University of Maryland.

2

While many cite the importance of having a mentor, focusing on the quality and nature of specific interactions between students and faculty can lead to better strategies promoting student agency. This chapter presents narratives from students who work with the same mentor, focusing on their interactions and how they shaped students' experiences and outcomes.

Digging Deeper: Exploring the Relationship Between Mentoring, Developmental Interactions, and Student Agency

Kimberly A. Griffin, Jennifer L. Eury, Meghan E. Gaffney, with Travis York, Jessica Bennett, Emil Cunningham, Autumn Griffin

Although it is often assumed that relationships between faculty and students will promote more positive educational outcomes, it has been challenging to identify what makes some mentoring relationships work better than others (O'Meara, Knudsen, & Jones, 2013). This is due, in part, to the fact that mentoring is a poorly defined construct. The distinctions between mentoring and other important developmental relationships such as advising, coaching, and serving as an advocate are rarely made (Baker & Griffin, 2010; Crisp & Cruz, 2009; Jacobi, 1991; Johnson, Rose, & Schlosser, 2010). Further, mentoring is often treated as a behavior in and of itself, although there is little consistency in how this behavior is or should be performed. This has translated to inconsistencies in academic research and difficulty establishing consistent connections between mentoring and student outcomes (Jacobi, 1991).

The purpose of this work is to add texture to our understanding of mentoring relationships, address the quality of interactions between students and faculty, and show how what happens within these relationships can relate to student outcomes. This is accomplished through close examination of the relationships among the authors of this chapter. Their scholarly personal narratives examining their mentoring relationships with one faculty member (Kimberly, the lead author) highlight the specific behaviors in which they engaged, and how these interactions related to their ability to

New Directions for Higher Education, no. 171, Fall 2015 © 2015 Wiley Periodicals, Inc.
Published online in Wiley Online Library (wileyonlinelibrary.com) • DOI: 10.1002/he.20138

reach their educational and career goals through the development of agency and purpose.

Background: Graduate Students and Agency

Agency can be defined as "assuming strategic perspectives and/or taking strategic actions towards goals that matter" (O'Meara, 2013, p. 2). Agency acknowledges the space between the power of social forces and individual decision making (Archer, 2000; Emirbayer & Mische, 1998), and focuses on the extent to which individuals feel they have the power to enact change and shape their own lives in a given context (Elder, 1994; O'Meara, 2013). O'Meara (2013) identifies two kinds of agency that are particularly relevant for graduate students: agentic perspectives and agentic actions. Having an agentic perspective addresses how an individual sees a situation, and whether the person perceives options or a role in creating his or her own reality and experience. Agentic action is related and often follows, focusing on behaviors "enacted with self-awareness of goals and contexts" (p. 3).

Agentic perspectives and actions are related to personal satisfaction, growth, and development (Archer, 2000; Emirbayer & Mische, 1998). Satisfaction, growth, and development may be particularly relevant for students as they face unfamiliar and challenging situations, make decisions about their careers, and strive to perform at the highest levels. While not always referred to as "agency," researchers have often shown the importance of feeling and exercising control over one's educational experiences (e.g., Hopwood, 2010; Lovitts, 2008; McAlpine & Amundsen, 2009). For example, faculty participating in Lovitts's research noted that successful graduate students were more willing to take control over their own research and learning. McAlpine and Amundsen also highlight the importance of student agency, noting that it must be modeled and encouraged to promote more positive student outcomes.

Rethinking Mentoring

O'Meara (2013) recommends mentoring as a way to promote graduate student agency, and encourages both deeper student understanding of what can be gained within these relationships and more faculty incentives to support student interaction. Limitations in extant literature and understandings of mentoring make this recommendation challenging to implement. There is little understanding about the nature of interactions between faculty members and students, what happens within relationships, and how specific interactions may be linked to student outcomes (Johnson et al., 2010; O'Meara et al., 2013). For example, Kram (1988) suggests that developmental relationships can serve multiple functions that, while not completely distinct, generally fall into two categories: career or psychosocial. A relationship focused on psychosocial functions, attending largely to building competence and identity, will likely entail a very different set of behaviors and interactions than a relationship that emphasizes career development and advancement.

Rather than assuming that all interactions are the same or focusing on whether students were mentored, our work emphasizes the importance of understanding "developmental interactions" (D'Abate, Eddy, & Tannenbaum, 2003), which represent both brief and long-term interactions that result in personal or professional development. This chapter examines the developmental interactions taking place between one faculty member and her students, focusing on specific behaviors and activities in which the students and faculty member engaged. This level of analysis allows for a deeper understanding of how mentors may facilitate certain student outcomes within their mentoring relationships, focusing specifically on agentic outcomes that promote student success.

Methods

Similar to Fries-Britt and Turner Kelly's (2005) examination of their own mentoring relationship, this chapter utilizes scholarly personal narrative due to its ability to highlight authors' voices and share their perceptions and interpretations of their lived experiences. Sharing one's story can reveal insights and depth not usually found in research, and can be a unique way to construct new knowledge (Nash, 2004).

Participants

The data for this project were drawn from scholarly personal narratives from students with whom the lead author, Kimberly, worked at the first institution at which she was employed. *Kimberly* is an African American woman who is an associate professor at a research university. Six current and former students (four women, two men) participated in the study: Autumn, Emil, Jennifer, Jessica, Meghan, and Travis.

Autumn is an African American woman who met Kimberly while she was a sophomore in college. She is now a sixth-grade teacher with Teach for America, and has an interest in pursuing graduate studies in the near future. *Emil* is an African American man who recently received his doctoral degree and aspires to become a senior student affairs officer. He met Kimberly as a master's student; she served as his doctoral program advisor and was a member of his dissertation committee. *Jennifer* is a White woman, recently completed her doctoral degree, and is also an administrator and instructor in the business college of a research university. Kimberly was her advisor before her departure from the institution. *Jessica* is a White, female doctoral candidate in higher education. She recently transferred to another research university, where Kimberly accepted a new position. *Meghan* is a White female student affairs professional at a research university. Kimberly

NEW DIRECTIONS FOR HIGHER EDUCATION • DOI: 10.1002/he

served as her master's degree program advisor. *Travis* is a new assistant professor of higher education. He is a White male, and Kimberly was on his dissertation committee.

Data Collection

Kimberly initiated the study with an invitation to the coauthors about writing an article reflecting on their perceptions, experiences, and educational outcomes as related to mentorship.

All coauthors were asked to submit scholarly personal narratives of approximately 500 words on their interactions with a mentor—in this case, Kimberly. Scholarly personal narratives are personal reflections, organized in intentional ways around specific themes or concepts (Nash, 2004). Thus, everyone was asked to: "Describe the nature of your relationship and interactions with Kimberly. Think and write about what you did and how your interactions and the activities in which you engaged within the relationship related to your efforts to reach your goals." Coauthors were provided with chapters from Nash's (2004) *Liberating Scholarly Writing: The Power of Personal Narrative*, for guidance on the process of writing their own narratives. After an initial review, some authors were recontacted to clarify or add to their narratives.

Data Analysis

In an effort to establish similarities and differences across the relationships formed and interactions between students and one specific faculty member, data were aggregated and coded, and are presented thematically rather than in a conversational format (e.g., Fries-Britt & Turner Kelly, 2005). The structure for data analysis loosely followed the guidelines for team-based analysis outlined by MacQueen, McLellan, Kay, & Milstein (1998), and the constant comparative method (Glaser & Strauss, 1967). Kimberly, along with Jennifer and Meghan (the two student lead authors), read and reread each narrative, memoing to capture their perceptions on themes that emerged from the data (Bogdan & Biklen, 1998). They then met to discuss their memos, including their perceptions of emerging themes. Groups of behaviors were identified, as well as resulting outcomes. The lead authors then discussed the connections between these behaviors, the mentoring literature, and student agency.

The emerging themes were translated to a list of codes, and applied to the data for analysis. The coding of the data was largely completed by Meghan, who edited and added to her preliminary codes, applied them to the data, and submitted them to the lead authors for review and use in developing the findings. Sections were drafted by Meghan and Jennifer, collectively discussed, and revised by Kimberly, revisiting the data to ensure that there was enough evidence to support each theme.

Findings

Each mentee entered into the mentoring relationship with Kimberly with specific areas of interest and different personal and professional goals in mind. For some, establishing and developing research skills were a priority. Jennifer "wanted to be actively involved in research projects." Autumn aimed "to gain as much research experience as I could during my undergraduate career," and Jessica "wanted to be thrown into the deep end of research." Similarly, Travis "was looking for a committee member who had experience with student outcomes and mixed methods" and "an opportunity to TA [be a teaching assistant] for a class related to students to round out my CV." Others centered on administrative career paths in student affairs. Meghan was "focused on defining my path in student affairs," and Emil, while initially committed to pursuing a position as a residence life director, now admitted "that my interactions with this woman [Kimberly] would completely alter my perspective on my chosen field."

While articulating different goals, analysis of the six scholarly personal narratives revealed three groups of behaviors that were consistent across the relationships and connected to the development of students' agency: approachability through psychosocial support, support and challenge, and development of professional voice. The final emerging theme, discovering purpose, speaks to the ways in which these groups of behaviors ultimately translated to students' outcomes.

Approachability Through Psychosocial Support

This section defines a brief, yet critical, connection between the perceived approachability of the mentor, the development of trust and comfort, and the cultivation of student agency. Most narratives described initial contact with Kimberly as surprising in its warmth, timeliness, and genuineness. Autumn shared, "I sent an e-mail expecting to be contacting some fire-breathing professor who would tell me they didn't have time to help an undergraduate facilitate her first research project. ... I received a warm and welcoming e-mail back." For some, Kimberly's approachability was familial, as Emil described: "I remember thinking that this woman was oddly and truly more genuine than I had expected. ... I experienced a bond that I have with many Black women in my family." For others, the relationship was defined by something more simple and overt, like a sense of style, booming laughter, or "soft tissues and dark chocolate" described by Meghan, who said, "The combination of personal care and academic encouragement further developed my self-efficacy."

No matter the circumstances used to initiate and build the relationship, the advisees all reflected on Kimberly's ability to make them feel comfortable, included, and valued in their personal and professional spheres. For Jessica, Autumn, and Jennifer, the experience was mostly framed in research. Emil, Travis, and Meghan described more unconditional support and friendship. Meghan wrote, "Kim made me feel significant. I faced a number of challenges during graduate school and she encouraged me the whole way. ... I never felt like an imposition reaching out." Each mentee saw a relationship between trusting Kimberly and developing the skills to work through challenges with competence and self-belief. Perhaps Travis summed it up best saying, "Kim became a mentor with whom I could share my best and worst ideas, doubts, insecurities, and triumphs while providing encouragement and guidance without condescension."

Challenge and Support

Analysis of the scholarly personal narratives suggests that the process by which Kimberly mentored was consistently grounded in challenge and support (Sanford, 1966). She challenged the students with new assignments and opportunities and even new perspectives, but provided support by way of encouragement and academic insight. Narratives suggest Kimberly assessed and individually addressed the specific needs. Her level of both support and challenge evolved over time, moving from each student's initial areas of interest to new opportunities for learning and development.

In her relationship with Jessica, for example, Kimberly challenged her to explore and try new opportunities. While other colleagues were "making copies and writing annotated bibliographies," she had autonomy and responsibility on shared projects. She noted, "At the start of every new project, manuscript, or semester, Kimberly asked me what I wanted to experience next, what activity I wanted to try, what role I wanted to play." Similarly, Kimberly challenged Autumn to get involved with a research project and "worked extremely hard to make sure that I was never singled out because of my age." Meghan also acknowledged that "Kimberly could never ask me enough questions," and challenged her to enroll in "difficult classes" to explore all of her areas of interest. While there were times when Meghan felt uneasy about pursuing course work outside of the program, Kimberly supported her in saying, "You're smart enough to do this. It's hard to be out of your comfort zone!"

By way of offering both challenge and support, Kimberly assumed an agentic perspective; her specific discussions with the mentees, as well as her recommendations, were strategic in nature. For some of the mentees, like Jennifer, Autumn, and Jessica, who were eager to embark on research, Kimberly offered one degree of challenge and support, and for other mentees, like Travis, who was eager to identify a full-time employment opportunity, she offered another degree of challenge and support. Drawing on O'Meara's (2013) application of agency, Kimberly was aware of individual differences, especially as they relate to students and professional goals, as well as the contexts of individual situations, and therefore strategically provided the relevant challenges and supports.

Encouraging Exploration and Supporting Development of Voice

The findings suggest that the mentees each gained greater understanding of their personal and/or professional identities, as well as a sense of voice, through Kimberly's efforts to encourage exploration. Jennifer recognized the challenges associated with at one point being both a part-time student and a full-time employee, while Autumn recognized the challenges related to being "the youngest and only undergraduate [student] on the research team." In both situations, Kimberly offered comfort and coaching to address Jennifer's academic and professional role identities and Autumn's ability to find a voice. For Meghan, Kimberly supported her desire to be seen as a scholar. In reinforcing her good work and encouraging her, she helped Meghan develop a sense of belonging as a student who was transitioning from part-time to full-time status. Kimberly supported Jessica in readjusting her goals of becoming a scholar-practitioner as she worked on her university's sexual assault prevention efforts. Emil credits "the opportunity to explore my own voice and believe that my opinion and perspective could be valued" to his decision to apply to and enroll in the PhD program. He revealed that his "interactions with Kimberly allowed me to overcome my insecurities as well as gain a sense of self-confidence." Travis and Kimberly had the opportunity to engage in lengthy discussions about identity development. For Travis, the validation he experienced in conversations about race, power, privilege, and oppression helped to move him into a realm of research that resonated with him. "I had always been passionate about these topics, but had felt like an outsider in terms of researching or teaching them. ... Kim encouraged me to pursue these passions in my research, and empowered my voice in that process."

Discovering Purpose

The mentees also described working through a unique pathway in their narratives. Each mentee identified a problem or question early on in the mentoring relationship, and made steady strides to address challenges or to create solutions that contributed to a sense of agency and accomplishment. In Meghan's case, Kimberly's mentorship encouraged her to explore different disciplines and truly understand the meaning of mentorship. Emil developed a similar appreciation for mentoring through his relationship, saying, "Kimberly saw in me the potential to be better than I imagined myself being." For Travis, the comforts of his friendship with Kimberly led to highly impactful discussions about power, privilege, and layers of identity. He wrote, "Kim didn't engage me, she engaged with me." Jennifer described feeling connected to her mentor through common research interests, which also created space for candid discussions about balancing personal and professional life. "I know there will continue to be challenges, but I am also working hard to celebrate my successes along the way, too—something that I also learned from Kim."

NEW DIRECTIONS FOR HIGHER EDUCATION • DOI: 10.1002/he

Conclusions and Implications

Archer (2003) states that assuming agentic perspective "means noticing constraints and potential opportunities, acting as a strong evaluator of situations, and then moving forward with a belief in choices and possibilities" (O'Meara, 2013, p. 3). By all accounts, Kimberly provided genuine relationships that enabled students to work through their constraints and opportunities, and supported them in weighing their options, either in real time or in preparation for the future. Developmental interactions that established accessibility and fostered trust, challenged students while providing instrumental and emotional support, and offered encouragement as students found and expressed their voices and individual interests formed strong foundations for students to find their own voices. Narratives demonstrated common themes regarding how a willingness to share resources, make time for them, and pose intentional questions can lead to psychosocial development. Discovery of purpose emerged as a core theme for all of the coauthors. Mentees felt comfortable with progress, partially because of the ways they were engaged in their mentoring relationships. Thus, in many ways, these behaviors could be understood as fostering their agency, particularly their respective agentic perspectives and perceived control over their own development and experiences.

In reviewing her mentees' narratives, Kimberly laughed at all of the similarities, saying, "I thought I was treating everyone differently, but it looks like my approach is the same!" Many of the behaviors in which the authors were engaging appear to reflect emotional intelligence as described by O'Meara et al. (2013). These authors note the importance of displays of personal and social competence by students and mentors in fostering strong relationships and positive student outcomes. Optimism (the assumption of success despite challenges), empathy (attention to others' emotions), and developing others (having an awareness of the needs and strengths of those who are being worked with) appeared particularly important to the students, as they connected behaviors that fell within these categories to their agency and development of purpose. Encouraging faculty to consider whether and how they are engaging in these behaviors may be particularly important, and providing faculty with professional development opportunities that identify these behaviors as important components of mentoring relationships would be a useful strategy to implement.

Finally, while the themes were consistent across the coauthors' narratives, it is important to note that the specific actions employed within each category varied across participants. This speaks to the need for faculty to adapt their behaviors to reflect not only their own strengths, but also the needs of their students. Not all students will have the same goals, seek the same opportunities, want to develop personal relationships, or respond well to the same ratio of challenge and support (Johnson, 2007). Thus, while the same fundamental principles may compose a faculty member's mentoring style, it is important to encourage and provide faculty members with opportunities to consider how they are applying those principles in each of their relationships and to tailor their developmental interactions in ways that promote distinct outcomes relevant to their students. Further, encouraging students to reflect on their needs and goals and to share them with their mentors can also promote better relationships, enabling faculty to engage in behaviors that best facilitate their growth and sense of agency.

References

Archer, M. S. (2000). *Being human: The problem of agency*. New York, NY: Cambridge University Press.

Archer, M. S. (2003). *Structure, agency, and the internal conversation*. New York, NY: Cambridge University Press.

Baker, V., & Griffin, K. A. (2010). Beyond mentoring and advising: Toward understanding the role of faculty "developers" in student success. *About Campus*, 14(6), 2–8.

Bogdan, R. C., & Biklen, S. K. (1998). *Qualitative research in education: An introduction to theory and methods* (3rd ed.). Boston, MA: Allyn & Bacon.

Crisp, G., & Cruz, I. (2009). Mentoring college students: A critical review of the literature between 1990 and 2007. *Research in Higher Education*, 50(6), 525–545. doi:10.1007/s11162-009-9130-2

D'Abate, C., Eddy, E. R., & Tannenbaum, S. I. (2003). What's in a name? A literature-based approach to understanding mentoring, coaching, and other constructs that describe developmental interactions. *Human Resource Development Review*, 2(4), 360–384.

Elder, G. H., Jr. (1994). Time, human agency, and social change: Perspectives on the life course. *Social Psychology Quarterly*, 57(1), 4–15.

Emirbayer, M., & Mische, A. (1998). What is agency? *American Journal of Sociology*, 103(4), 962–1023.

Fries-Britt, S., & Turner Kelly, B. T. (2005). Retaining each other: Narratives of two African American women in the academy. *Urban Review*, 37(3), 221–242.

Glaser, B. G., & Strauss, A. L. (1967). *The discovery of grounded theory: Strategies for qualitative research*. Chicago, IL: Aldine.

Hopwood, N. (2010). A sociocultural view of doctoral students' relationships and agency. *Studies in Continuing Education*, 32(2), 103–117.

Jacobi, M. (1991). Mentoring and undergraduate academic success: A literature review. *Review of Educational Research*, 61(4), 505–532.

Johnson, B. J. (2007). *On being a mentor: A guide for higher education faculty*. New York, NY: Psychology Press, Taylor & Francis Group.

Johnson, B. J., Rose, G., & Schlosser, L. Z. (2010). Student-faculty mentoring: Theoretical and methodological issues. In T. D. Allen & L. T. Eby (Eds.), *The Blackwell handbook of mentoring: A multiple perspectives approach* (pp. 49–69). Malden, MA: Blackwell.

Kram, K. E. (1988). *Mentoring at work: Developmental relationships in organizational life*. Lanham, MD: University Press of America.

Lovitts, B. E. (2008). The transition to independent research: Who makes it and why. *Journal of Higher Education*, 79(3), 296–325.

MacQueen, K. M., McLellan, E., Kay, K., & Milstein, B. (1998). Codebook development for team based qualitative analysis. *Cultural Anthropology Methods*, 10(2), 31–36.

McAlpine, L., & Amundsen, C. (2009). Identity and agency: Pleasures and collegiality among the challenges of the doctoral journey. *Studies in Continuing Education, 31*(2), 109–125.

Nash, R. J. (2004). *Liberating scholarly writing: The power of personal narrative.* New York, NY: Teachers College Press.

O'Meara, K. (2013). Advancing graduate student agency. *Higher Education in Review, 10,* 1–10.

O'Meara, K., Knudsen, K., & Jones, J. (2013). The role of emotional competencies in faculty-doctoral student relationships. *Review of Higher Education, 36*(3), 315–347.

Sanford, N. (1966). *Self and society.* New York, NY: Atherton Press.

KIMBERLY A. GRIFFIN, PhD, is an associate professor in the College of Education at the University of Maryland, and director of the student affairs academic program in the Department of Counseling, Higher Education, and Special Education.

JENNIFER L. EURY, PhD, is the honor and integrity director and instructor in management at the Smeal College of Business at the Pennsylvania State University.

MEGHAN E. GAFFNEY, MEd, is the associate director of fraternity and sorority life at the University of Pennsylvania.

NEW DIRECTIONS FOR HIGHER EDUCATION • DOI: 10.1002/he

3

This chapter outlines critical practices that emerged from utilizing social justice frameworks to mentor first-generation, underrepresented minority students at the undergraduate to doctoral levels. The mentoring strategies include helping students to reframe instances when faculty and peers unconsciously conflate academic rigor with color-blind scholarship.

Critical Mentoring Practices to Support Diverse Students in Higher Education: Chicana/Latina Faculty Perspectives

Julie López Figueroa, Gloria M. Rodriguez

Advising fundamentally centers on making sure students gain awareness of and meet their academic requirements, whereas mentoring brokers professional development about how current preparation positions oneself for future careers after graduation. Ideally, advising and mentoring coexist as integrated practice and are offered to all students equally. Expectedly, we advise and mentor students in our respective fields, ethnic studies and education. In addition, our work with undergraduate and graduate students has revealed countless mentoring conversations with Latina/o students beyond our own disciplines, including biology, engineering, English, history, mathematics, political science, sociology, and various subfields in education.

Although there is an operating assumption that one primary responsibility of faculty is to mentor students, our observations of student experience reveal how mentoring is a racially and culturally mediated experience instead of a race-neutral, objective interaction. The experiences of mentoring students of color outside of our disciplinary training have raised some deep concerns about what is not happening for students in their own fields. Also illuminated were possible strategies that in the long run could enrich faculty advising practices and strongly support students' professional development.

This chapter begins with a brief discussion that situates the act of mentoring within the landscape of higher education. In doing so, we also present our own positionalities as mentors, including the stances that we maintain and negotiate in our practice, to make explicit for readers how we view the

NEW DIRECTIONS FOR HIGHER EDUCATION, no. 171, Fall 2015 © 2015 Wiley Periodicals, Inc.
Published online in Wiley Online Library (wileyonlinelibrary.com) • DOI: 10.1002/he.20139

nature of academia and our location within it. Second, we utilize a social justice framing of our mentoring practice, namely, drawing upon the conceptual formulations of Gloria E. Anzaldúa (2002), Paulo Freire (1993), and Tara J. Yosso (2005). Third, we outline some of the politics of mentoring students of color as faculty of color. Fourth, we highlight mentoring student experiences using the approaches we describe. Finally, we offer some guiding principles that we extract from our mentoring practices.

Situating Mentoring Within Higher Education and Ourselves as Mentors

Can mentoring engulfed within a meritocratic culture be a race-neutral experience for Latina/o students? We speculate that the underrepresentation of faculty of color in combination with the ongoing adherence to the principle of "merit" in higher education (Contreras, 2005) creates a challenging atmosphere for Latino undergraduate and graduate students, who trustingly assume that all faculty members in their programs would be personally invested in the students' success and well-being. To understand faculty–student mentoring relationships, we must recognize that meritocracy shapes practices, traditions, norms, and language in higher education.

Meritocracy operates purportedly as an independent, neutral, and objective ideological vehicle for governing and educating college students (Altbach & Lomotey, 1991; Tatum, 1997; Yosso, 2005). Presumably, learning and teaching are dispensed through a color-blind approach where excellence is cast as race-neutral, individualistic success (Contreras, 2005; Delgado Bernal, 1999). Entrenched within what is considered a "normal routine" (Sue, 2004, 2005), however, reside unexamined attitudes and practices, which is where institutionalized racism remains invisible to many, unchanging, and perpetuated (Sue, 2005). Though not personally intended, institutionalized racism is far from incidental when meritocracy is one inherited, unchallenged element still operating within higher education (Altbach & Lomotey, 1991).

Within this milieu, we continuously reflect upon our positionality as faculty members who likewise bring to the environment our own complex mix of experiences and identities. The biggest conflict—that between our core values and those of the institution of academia—warrants reflection upon each of our social locations and our decision to participate in such a hegemonic, exclusionary, and hostile profession. Each of us brings our own set of lived experiences, which inform how we carry out our mentoring practices. Likewise, the perspectives we have about college and graduate school also reflect each of our experiences with navigating those environments prior to becoming faculty members. Therefore, we wish to be explicit in stating that our experiences in and perspectives on higher education are infused in the ways we convey feedback, collaborate in sense-making processes with our mentees, and engage in truth-telling as a feature of demystifying the academic socialization/racialization process.

We offer this consideration of our positionality to readers as a way to articulate that our mentoring practice is as challenged by the pressures to conform to and the need to push back on the traditions of academia as we observe our students' experiences to be. However, we do not consider our worldviews to be universal. So, we proceed in our practice with the consciousness that our work is not to simply reproduce ourselves through our students' development but rather to embrace the complexity of what our students represent and join in the negotiation of their/our perspectives and stances together. To clarify this approach a bit further, we discuss next our use of a social justice framing of our mentoring practice.

Mentoring as Social Justice Work in Higher Education: Drawing From Anzaldúa, Freire, and Yosso

As we take a moment to consider the nature of our mentoring practice, we identify several thematic descriptors of our intentions and pursuits that emerge in our work with Chicana/Latina students: emancipatory and reflective practice, consciousness development, reclaiming of one's history and personal power, and individual and collective agency. Gloria E. Anzaldúa's (2002) focus on the development of one's critical consciousness or *conocimiento*—particularly as she encourages us to embrace our vulnerabilities as a source of understanding, engage in creative productivity, and strive to articulate our multiple (and at times conflicting) identities—is key for our work as Chicana mentors of our Chicana/Latina students. In all her writings, Anzaldúa invites each of us on a journey of self-discovery that is rooted in beliefs, values, and political stances that reflect in important ways the personal and political identities of the students with whom we work, as well as our own. In one particular essay, "Now Let Us Shift ... the Path of Conocimiento ... Inner Work, Public Acts," Anzaldúa (2002)[1] describes the need to consider the borders that are constantly crossed as we pursue deeper understanding and wisdom about ourselves and the world around us, which is instructive for examining the challenges of combining our political identities as Chicanas with the professional identities of scholars and educators. *Nepantla* is the term that Anzaldúa offers to help us articulate the types of upheaval that are part of developing a process of navigating, negotiating, and synthesizing our lived experiences to clarify our stances as human beings involved in collaborative knowledge production. Indeed, in this essay she provides scenarios very close to home for us as mentors:

> There's only one Chicana in your Ph.D. program at UT Austin, Texas, a state heavily populated with Chicanos, and you're never in the same class. The professors dislike the practice of putting yourself in the texts, insisting your

papers are too subjective. They frown on your unorthodox perspectives and ways of knowing. They reject your dissertation thesis, claiming Chicana/o literature illegitimate and feminist theory too radical. (p. 548)

By drawing on Anzaldúa, we are able to reflect upon our mentoring practice as an opportunity to create the safe spaces for our students to utilize these moments of social, cultural, and intellectual isolation as additional sources of consciousness-building and development that embrace multiple forms of knowledge and epistemologies—even as we broker opportunities for their professional advancement within the traditional, constrained pathways to success as young scholars.

The manner by which our students and we do our academic work is also resonant with the encouragement by Paulo Freire to center in our analyses the perspectives of those who live in the inequitable conditions we seek to understand and change. Moreover, Freire insists that we conduct reflective work that will make a positive difference in the world around us— engage in *praxis*. Similar to the goals pursued by Anzaldúa,[2] Freire's (1993) *Pedagogy of the Oppressed* outlines a collaborative knowledge production process that facilitates a critical consciousness-building effort (conscientization), as well as a reclaiming of one's humanity in the process. Indeed, a facile treatment of the traditional academic realm on our part could easily occur, in which we foster in our students an attitude of rejection of all that is not familiar and close to our personal, social, and historical contexts as Chicanas/Latinas, especially those of us who claim working-class roots and great social distance from the unearned privilege replete in academia.

However, Freire's work instead challenges us to understand the inextricable relationship between the oppressed and the oppressors and cautions us to remember the cost to both when we perpetuate through our own practices systems that negate our humanity. In this regard, Freire's discussion of the banking method of teaching-learning is an important prompt for our work as mentors in that we must remain vigilant to share what we have learned about being in academia *thus far* while also maintaining an openness to the fact that our students each bring their own lived experience and are pursuing their own journeys through academia—not merely reproducing ours or blindly accepting our truths as theirs. This further translates into our embracing the convictions of our students who seek to make a difference in the world through their research—often starting with their hometowns or settings quite similar—as opposed to pushing them to extricate such stances from their beings in service of becoming the ideal, disinterested researchers. In other words, we mentor *and* are mentored by our students.

Finally, our mentoring practice is informed by Tara J. Yosso's (2005) community cultural wealth framework as a manifestation of the historical and contemporary practices that are rooted in lessons drawn from adversity, resistance, and aspirations that defy the cultural deficit characterizations (Valencia, 1997) of their/our families and communities. In addition, just as Yosso (2006) emphasizes a critical race theory–informed analysis of the sociopolitical conditions under which Chicana/os and Latina/os pursue higher education, we find it useful to apply this framework to our mentoring practice because through this lens we are able to understand the depths of racialization that occur in our students' navigations of the university context. Yosso's use of counterstories, in particular, provides an instructive strategy for co-constructing with our students explanatory theories for the persistence of inequities that shift our view from the academy's tendency toward individualistic formulations of success and failure to a more systemic view of how the business as usual of uninterrogated entitlement, privilege, and institutionalized bias function to marginalize our students and their communities. This is not to say that we mentor our students to offer counterarguments that cast themselves only as victims of institutionalized oppression, since this would be an irresponsible tactic on our part, as so thoughtfully explicated by Tatum (1997). Rather, we draw upon Yosso's community cultural wealth framework and counterstorytelling to (re)activate the personal and community assets of our students that are born from inequitable situations but that nevertheless provide them with a set of strategies, epistemologies, and resistant convictions that move us past simplistic notions of resilience and motivation as sources of personal power and well-being.

The Politics of Mentoring: A Tradition of Faculty Self-Interest or a Practice of Responsiveness?

Depending on the campus, mentoring opportunities may range in structure from formal to informal arrangements. While the strength and momentum of this relationship hinge on the mutual investment by the mentor and mentee, there is the belief that the mentor will take the lead in facilitating the experience. A common mentoring structure is the expert who scaffolds understanding for the novice—a type of banking method (Freire, 1993) for mentors. Whereas advising is a formal arrangement through which a student comes to know "how to do school," mentoring is more about developing professional know-how and well-being. Mentoring promotes the very best of one's profession through illuminating a process of knowledge production and productivity. Mentoring is a professional development relationship meant to demystify, enrich, and stretch one's thinking about how to be an effective scholar, model collegiality, and frame one's work as a useful resource to those outside the university.

Faculty mentors broker opportunities for students to contextualize advice, assist students to develop insights, and offer guidance on how to strive for excellence in a given field. Working from this foundation, two questions come to mind: What are some key issues that mediate the mentoring experiences of Latina/o students within a meritocratic culture? What are some high-impact mentoring practices to consider when working with Latina/o students? Perhaps due to tenure-related expectations and pressures, never having been taught to value diversity considerations in their discipline as graduate students, or adherence to the belief that diversity does not enrich a knowledge base, such faculty members seek solely an intellectual match before committing to mentoring a student. Other times, faculty members with less experience mentoring students of color justify diminishing or devaluing diversity out of the belief that academic rigor means preserving the traditional academic canon, rather than recognizing its potential limitations for integrating diverse worldviews. Such mentoring, according to Rendón (2009), suggests the enactment of a "separatist view of teaching and learning [that] works to detach the student from what is being learned. Whatever learning takes place has little to do with the learning; the learning is 'out there,' independent of the student" (p. 35). Moreover, mentoring through self-interest may be efficient for a traditionally trained tenure-track faculty member, but it may inadvertently transform mentoring into a racializing experience. Certainly, we recognize that the fundamentals in a discipline serve as an important foundation. However, mentoring by doing nothing beyond preserving the canon requires excluding diverse perspectives through narrowing epistemological approaches versus challenging or extending the canon through innovative knowledge production with our mentees.

Although it can definitely be said that Latina/o students may find allies among White faculty, and that not all faculty of color may be supportive of Latino/a students, the disproportionate underrepresentation of Latina/o faculty compared to their White counterparts warrants some consideration regarding the ways mentoring can become a racialized experience (Omi & Winant, 1994; Sue, 2005) for Latina/o students. This is especially true when faculty may hold the belief that some students from certain racial/ethnic groups are more competent than others (Norman & Norman, 1995). Without personal reflection, personal accountability, and personal investment toward promoting or incorporating diversity into the mentoring, our colleagues risk the perpetuation of cultural deficit thinking.

Our Mentoring Experiences as Chicana/Latina Faculty

As mentors, we supportively supplement and enrich the sense-making processes of students within our respective campuses and in relationship to various benchmark activities, such as choosing a major, understanding graduation requirements, selecting a research topic for a McNair project or graduate dissertation, applying for internships and scholarships, or preparing an application for an academic position. While there is tremendous focus on reading, writing, and critical thinking, as faculty and mentors we attempt to rehumanize as well as build upon what students bring. Students routinely express to us their interest in researching phenomena affecting their lives. These personal connections to their work often become an important entry point for us to engage in our mentoring practices. Next, we share our interactions with students to help illuminate how this work actually plays out.

Figueroa.   During my first year of teaching, I taught a course on Chicana feminism. The final assignment required students to produce a research paper to explore Chicana identity in their lives. With only two of the 40 students familiar with writing a research project, I explained the processes for constructing a title, formulating a research question, and writing an annotated bibliography. To ignite enthusiasm, students were encouraged to choose a topic of personal interest to create a meaningful experience. One of the Chicana students came to my office to explain that she had difficulty coming up with an interesting topic.

Remembering her dance performance on campus, I suggested she theorize and articulate the everyday reality of constructing identity through ballet *folklórico* in connection with Chicana feminism. She gave me an incredulous stare and stated, "I can really do that? Really? I didn't think I could because it's about my life." She could hardly believe that her lived experience could merit any sort of academic analysis. Although met with great skepticism, I reminded this student that Chicana feminism recognizes the daily experience as a site of knowledge production. With this idea in mind, we discussed her decision to engage and prioritize *folklórico* amid potential family politics specifically and gender politics in general. Additionally, with magazines or commercials imposing standards of beauty around body image, ballet *folkórico* enabled her to construct a cultural narrative that resonated with her world. By the end of our conversation, this Chicana felt less challenged, went on to complete the project successfully, and ultimately received a graduate degree in counseling. If the academic canon is incapable of recognizing the value of people, then mentors must bring clarity and extend knowledge.

Rodriguez.   My example of my mentoring practice is one that actually also involves my colleague and coauthor of this chapter. A few years ago, after feeling inundated with the requests for support from multiple advisees (and adoptees) and also hearing myself repeating the same advice several times in a given week, I decided to establish a seminar that would allow me to better streamline my work with my advisees. I patterned my seminar, "Applied Research with Chicana/o-Latina/o Communities," after UCLA colleague Daniel Solórzano's Research Apprenticeship course, and I conduct it as a group research course, which allows me to offer it to students for varying units of credit. Together, we co-construct this counterspace (Yosso, 2006) of intellectual, academic, and personal growth that is grounded in a shared commitment to critical consciousness development.

A typical session involves our reading and critiquing of students' writing—the range includes conference papers, qualifying exam papers, draft articles for publication, and so forth—using layered forms of feedback that I employ to attend to the various dimensions of the students' experience whenever possible. In other words, I ensure that we attend to the rigor of the students' writing, their arguments, their presentation of literature or evidence to back their claims, and their use of various theoretical lenses to inform their analyses. However, I (and various faculty colleagues I may invite) also take up issues that arise in the production of the work, such as the Chicana/Latina researchers' ethics in engaging Latina/o community members as participants in their research and offering supportive advice on how to maintain respect for the boundaries around people's lives, which our students often intuitively invoke, given their own past experiences as "the researched" (Figueroa & Sánchez, 2005). Note that this more collaborative stance as researchers challenges the privileged positions they occupy as emerging scholars who are trained to be *entitled to know* by virtue of their roles and academic objectives.

Critical Mentoring Practices as Social Justice Work: Some Guiding Principles

We are compelled to take a step back from our own mentoring practices to offer a few guiding principles that emerge, but we are also quick to remind readers (once again) that we do not view our perspectives as universal. We offer this set of guiding principles for successful mentoring practices used with our Latina/o students but caution against viewing it as a checklist. Rather, we share these guiding principles as a way to articulate some touchstones that have worked in our contexts and in our shared journey as mentors of amazing, talented, brilliant, and still astonishingly marginalized Chicana/Latina students in higher education. In keeping with our application of Anzaldúa, Freire, and Yosso, we affirm that we have learned from our mentees as much as or more than we have taught them about what it means—and what it takes—to successfully navigate and negotiate the hegemonic environment that is academe. Our hope is that the following guiding principles may serve as a starting point for reflection and dialogue about our roles as mentors in higher education:

1. *Critical consciousness-building is our goal.* Both in the academic pursuits and in the personal/professional development realm, we attend to the complexity of who we and our students are within and beyond academia so as to facilitate a more holistic analysis of the impact and meaning of our intellectual work as Chicana/Latina scholars and educators.

2. *Lived experience matters.* We often take time to remind our mentees of who they are, based not on our assessments but on their own narratives that they shared when we all first met, including our reading of their applications to our programs. In the spirit of truth-telling, we use lived experience—our own, that of our students, and that of their/our family and community members—as a crucial reminder of where we have been and what it has taken to get to this point in our

lives and work. It is remarkable how easily the memory of and the value placed on lived experience is lost in the context of academic pressures to conform and adhere to dominant ways of knowing.

3. *We are champions for our mentees.* Our starting point when our students encounter challenges is not the assumption that they can't cut the mustard or perhaps were never "graduate school material" to begin with. We run interference by advocating on their behalf with our colleagues and/or we push students to seek out assistance from those with the appropriate expertise. However, we never stop believing that they are capable of being empowered, self-determined, whole human beings who will bring needs *and* strengths to the table.

Notes

1. Rodriguez wishes to thank Professors Inés Hernández-Avila (University of California, Davis) and Alicia Gaspar de Alba (UCLA) for introducing this essay to her as a means for reflecting upon her practice as a Chicana professor.

2. There are significant differences in the grounded perspectives of these two philosophers/scholars, certainly, which are beyond the scope of this article but warrant acknowledgment here nonetheless.

References

Altbach, P. G., & Lomotey, K. (1991). *The racial crisis in American higher education.* Albany, NY: State University of New York Press.

Anzaldúa, G. E. (2002). Now let us shift … the path of conocimiento … inner work, public acts. In G. E. Anzaldúa & A. Keating (Eds.), *This bridge we call home: Radical visions for transformation* (pp. 540–578). New York, NY: Routledge.

Contreras, F. (2005, May). The reconstruction of merit post-Proposition 209. *Educational Policy, 19*(2), 371–395.

Delgado Bernal, D. (1999). Chicana/o education from the civil rights era to the present. In J. F. Moreno (Ed.), *The elusive quest for equality: 150 years of Chicano/Chicana education* (pp. 77–110). Cambridge, MA: Harvard Educational Review.

Figueroa, J. L., & Sánchez, P. (2005). Technique, art, or cultural practice? Ethnic epistemology in Latino qualitative studies. In T. Fong (Ed.), *Research methods in ethnic studies* (pp. 143–178). Walnut Creek, CA: AltaMira Press.

Freire, P. (1993). *Pedagogy of the oppressed.* New York, NY: Continuum Publishing Company.

Norman, K. F., & Norman, J. E. (1995). The synergy of minority student performance and faculty renewal. *Innovative Higher Education, 20*(2), 129–140.

Omi, M., & Winant, H. (1994). *Racial formation in the United States: From the 1960s to the 1990s* (2nd ed.). New York, NY: Routledge.

Rendón, L. I. (2009). *Sentipensante (sensing/thinking) pedagogy: Educating for wholeness, social justice and liberation.* Sterling, VA: Stylus.

Sue, D. W. (2004). Whiteness and ethnocentric monoculturalism: Making the invisible visible. *American Psychologist, 59,* 759–769.

Sue, D. W. (2005). Racism and the conspiracy of silence. *Counseling Psychologist, 33*(1), 100–114.

Tatum, B. D. (1997). *Why are all the Black kids sitting together in the cafeteria? And other conversations about race.* New York, NY: Basic Books.

Valencia, R. (Ed.). (1997). *The evolution of deficit thinking: Educational thought and practice.* New York, NY: Routledge.

Yosso, T. J. (2005). Whose culture has capital? A critical race theory discussion of community cultural wealth. *Race, Ethnicity, and Education, 8*(2), 69–91.

Yosso, T. J. (2006). *Critical race counterstories along the Chicana/Chicano educational pipeline.* New York, NY: Routledge.

JULIE LÓPEZ FIGUEROA *is an associate professor at California State University, Sacramento, in the Department of Ethnic Studies.*

GLORIA M. RODRIGUEZ *is an associate professor at the University of California, Davis, in the School of Education.*

NEW DIRECTIONS FOR HIGHER EDUCATION • DOI: 10.1002/he

4

This chapter chronicles the use of educational testimonio *as one approach to critical pedagogy as mentoring in a college classroom. Written from the perspectives of an instructor and a student, it explores educational* testimonio *as one tool that has implications beyond the classroom, including retention in higher education and supporting the development of aspirations beyond undergraduate schools on the path to the professoriate.*

Educational *Testimonio*: Critical Pedagogy as Mentorship

Rebeca Burciaga, Natalia Cruz Navarro

Paulo Freire's (1970/1998) concept of *conscientização*—or the process of identifying and taking action against social injustice—requires self-reflection for social transformation. In the study of education, people often make critical decisions and assertions about issues in schools and communities without asking difficult questions such as: What are the principles that inform my views on educational opportunity as they relate to race, ethnicity, class, gender, citizenship status, language, or sexual orientation? How has my personal history helped me arrive at these principles (de los Reyes, 1998)? In studying educational inequities, one must deconstruct one's place within them. This is not a linear task but rather a process of speaking and writing oneself into clarity; a *testimonio* is one approach to this end.

Testimonio, a critical Latin American oral tradition practice, privileges and is contingent upon personal and communal experiences as important sources of knowledge in understanding one's place within political, social, and cultural contexts (Delgado Bernal, Burciaga, & Flores Carmona, 2012; Gutiérrez, 2008; Latina Feminist Group, 2001; Negron-Gonzales, 2009; Partnoy, 2006). As a "source of knowledge, empowerment, and political strategy for claiming rights and bringing about social change" (Benmayor, Torruellas, & Juarbe, 1997, p. 153), a *testimonio* is an epistemology of the storyteller.

In the spring of 2008, Natalia (an undergraduate transfer student) took a course with Rebeca (postdoctoral scholar/instructor) and wrote an educational *testimonio*—an autoethnographic-style research paper tracing one's individual educational trajectory through a mixed-methods approach by

NEW DIRECTIONS FOR HIGHER EDUCATION, no. 171, Fall 2015 © 2015 Wiley Periodicals, Inc.
Published online in Wiley Online Library (wileyonlinelibrary.com) • DOI: 10.1002/he.20140

contextualizing educational experiences alongside current research. Natalia recalls how her educational *testimonio* provided an opportunity to revisit and transcend traumatic experiences in schools. Through (re)analyzing experiences through a critical sociopsychological lens, she began to see opportunities for improving educational opportunities of students of color. Her belief that we must be "critical of our own journey and the role that we play in reinforcing ideologies that can be either oppressive or empowering" is one she currently embodies as a professional social worker. Written from two perspectives, those of an instructor and a student, this chapter explores educational *testimonio* as one approach to critical pedagogy as mentorship in the classroom with implications for inspiring civic engagement beyond institutions of higher education.

Finding Our Voices, Finding *Testimonio*

In the spirit of *testimonio*, we share who we are as individuals and how we came together for this work. First, Rebeca shares her background and journey toward *testimonio* as pedagogy. Second, Natalia describes her background and experiences writing an educational *testimonio*.

Rebeca: Finding *Testimonio*.   I am an assistant professor of educational leadership at San José State University. I attended the University of California at Santa Cruz (UCSC) and the Harvard Graduate School of Education, and received my PhD in education from the University of California, Los Angeles. I am the daughter of Cecilia Preciado Burciaga and José Antonio Burciaga, two first-generation Chicanos and college graduates—political activists in higher education and the arts throughout various political movements.

My schooling began in the home. Discussions of race, ethnicity, and culture were more common in my home than in my classroom. Not until graduate school did I participate in a classroom discussion or assignment about personal, political, and intellectual influences on my upbringing. I was asked to write a "political autobiography" for a course titled Education for Social and Political Change (T128) at the Harvard Graduate School of Education. Despite my background in ethnic studies, this was my introduction to Freirian pedagogy (Freire, 1970/1998). The class discussed readings alongside personal accounts—policies experienced by English language learners and accounts of being punished for speaking Spanish in school, for example. This assignment pushed me to reflect on my educational trajectory by unveiling privileges and interrogating everyday actions toward a social justice approach to schooling. Central to this activity were various mentors throughout my schooling—caring and nonjudgmental guides—who exposed me to critical theories and pedagogies that included various perspectives (Gutiérrez, 2008; Solorzano, 1989).

Even with wonderful graduate school mentors, I questioned my future in academia. As a woman of color in education, I was aware of the

NEW DIRECTIONS FOR HIGHER EDUCATION • DOI: 10.1002/he

narrow educational pathways to the professoriate and the health costs many paid to obtain tenure. I looked to critical scholar-pedagogues (Gutiérrez y Muhs, Flores Niemann, González, & Harris, 2012; Latina Feminist Group, 2001). These collections of narratives reignited my belief in reflection and dialogue. Their unapologetic discussions of how their life pathways were influenced by social, cultural, and historical intricacies of race, ethnicity, gender, immigration status, and sexuality in the United States affirmed my social justice work in the academy. I began to see experiential knowledge synonymous with students' intellectual resources. From the concept of funds of knowledge (Gonzalez, Moll, & Amanti, 2005) to community cultural wealth (Yosso, 2005), scholars are becoming increasingly attentive to the often-overlooked yet vast resources that students bring to educational settings. Without critical approaches to cultivating such resources, however, we lose opportunities to build community through learning from others' varying perspectives on the world. Moreover, the pathway to the professoriate is carved through socialization practices that include knowledge creation. *Testimonio* is one approach to socialization through an analysis of one's experiences as a foundation for aspirations that may seem out of reach for first-generation college students.

Assigning an Educational Testimonio.   I first used *testimonio* as my dissertation methodology for exploring Chicana PhD students' experiences from preschool to the professoriate (Burciaga, 2007). I understood *testimonio*'s pedagogical potential for college classrooms. I was given an opportunity to pilot *testimonio* as pedagogy as a postdoctoral scholar at the University of California, Santa Cruz (UCSC). The seminar, Latina/o Education in the United States: Social Policies, Individual Educational Development, and Contexts of Change, enrolled 12 students. Ten of the 12 enrollees were students of color and had transferred from community colleges. With a focus on schooling conditions and opportunities to learn for Latina/o students, my undergraduate seminar critically examined theories, research, and policies on educational attainment trends. Emphasis was placed on the organization and allocation of learning opportunities in schools and the importance of asset-based familial, cultural, and social resources in improving educational equity for Latina/o students. Students in the seminar were asked to write an educational *testimonio*—a paper that traced their own educational development (from childhood through adolescence and emerging adulthood) through a mixed-methods approach that contextualized their individual educational development in comparison with patterns highlighted by social science theories, quantitative data from national public data sets, and relevant social policies. The educational *testimonio* resulted in a 15- to 20-page paper but was written in three stages throughout the course.

The first stage of the educational *testimonio* began with students' reflections on their schooling experiences. In the second stage, students were asked to conduct original research using the Civil Rights Data

Collection to investigate resource allocation. Natalia, for example, researched the racial/ethnic composition of her high school in comparison with racial/ethnic enrollment in advanced placement courses. Students then analyzed their personal memoirs alongside discussions, readings, and their original research. The final educational *testimonio* blended the personal memoir, research data, and readings and discussions from the class. Students were then asked to give 15-minute presentations of their educational *testimonios* to their peers. At each stage, students provided various points of discussion in and out of class when the instructor met with students individually. These practices prompted shifts in knowledge production and dissemination from teacher/text only to student/*testimonio* in our learning community.

Over the years, many alumni—including Natalia—have written to share how this assignment contributed not only to their understanding of Latina/o educational attainment, but also to their own trajectories through college, informing their aspirations. Just after Natalia enrolled in her master's program, she expressed interest in pursuing a doctorate and exploring the possibility of an academic career.

Natalia: Finding *Testimonio*.   My name is Natalia Cruz Navarro. I am the daughter of Ignacio and Teresa, the sister of Jose Lorenzo, Jose de Jesus, and Teresa. I was born in Mexico and at the age of 9 immigrated to California in the United States, where I have since resided. I am currently working as a post-master's clinical social work trainee in Northern California. I am an alumna of the College of the Sequoias, University of California at Santa Cruz (UCSC), and San José State University, where I received my master's degree in social work.

As a first-generation community college transfer student and psychology major at UCSC, I found my experiences as a student of color to be seen as foreign, and invisible to those different from me. Coming from a low-income, immigrant, rural community in the Central Valley of California, my visibility and presence within the university—and more specifically, the classroom—greatly depended on the caring relationships that I forged with my professors and other mentors who guided me throughout college. Rebeca was, and has continued to be, one of these extraordinary mentors in my life.

Prior to enrolling in Rebeca's course, I had completed my junior year of undergraduate studies at UCSC, a year comprised of many moments marked by feelings of inadequacy, guilt, anxiety, and confusion, and constant self-imposed pressure to survive. Through the assignment and close mentorship, I was able to reflect on my college experience, validate my personal experience in college, and name the emotions that I had struggled to define. These feelings can best be explained by three themes commonly researched and identified by other college students of color: (1) impostor syndrome (Clance & Imes, 1978); (2) survivor's guilt (Yosso, 2006); and (3) resistance (Solorzano & Delgado Bernal, 2001).

My first encounter with impostor syndrome occurred fairly early on in my academic career at UCSC. Upon learning that I had been admitted, I was initially happy and excited to be joining this well-regarded academic institution. Shortly after I moved on campus to start the academic year, however, I began to feel like an impostor waiting to be caught—as though someone from the admissions office would eventually realize that I had been admitted to the university in error and that I had accidentally been granted a more deserving student's spot. Unfortunately, my assumption was supported by a shared sense of invisibility among my peers. This further led me to believe that I was admitted to this university only to fulfill a much-needed quota, the token Latina student.

My experience with survivor's guilt emerged when I gained entrance into UCSC. Although I was born into a family that had strong, hardworking, and determined role models, who in the face of adversity managed to envision and pursue a better life for their children, I found myself suddenly feeling guilty for being the first person in my immediate and extended family to make it into college. At one point, I remember realizing that I was the only one of my high school and community college friends who was enrolled in a 4-year institution. At the time, I felt as though I should leave UCSC so I could help my parents financially, because being a college student felt foreign and uncertain, and most of the time, it was almost unimaginable that this degree could bring any real value to my family and my future. Fortunately, my parents convinced me—as they always had—that my education was more important than anything else. I further learned in Rebeca's class—through our assigned readings, group discussions, one-on-one meetings, and my peers' experiences—that I had not been the only one who experienced survivor's guilt. This realization helped me broaden my understanding of the issues affecting students of color in general and the importance that we build coalitions among us. I continue to draw from this information in understanding the common experiences of children, adolescents, and families of color whom I currently serve in my work as a social worker.

In my psychology courses, I heard many stereotypical assumptions about communities of color. I rarely questioned these perceptions and found myself listening to many lectures and discussions among peers about communities of color that were based on the "deficit model" (Valencia & Black, 2002). For example, instructors and students made sweeping generalizations about the correlations between the challenges that children of color face and their parents' levels of education. This oversimplified explanation implied that parents of color—because they were not formally educated and did not speak English—were incapable of educating their children, involving themselves in their children's learning, or helping their children academically. While I intellectually accepted this concept as truth based on known facts of Latino high school dropout rates, my intuition suggested a more complex understanding of this phenomenon. I learned that there are multiple ways that Latina/o parents participate that are not recognized by

NEW DIRECTIONS FOR HIGHER EDUCATION • DOI: 10.1002/he

schools (Zarate, 2007) and multiple understandings of education (Valenzuela, 1999). Being a well-schooled person does not make a better parent. My parents do not have college degrees but were educated in a different manner. As Valenzuela argues, *educación* does not hold the same significance as its English counterpart, education. *Educación* refers "to the family's role of inculcating in children a sense of moral, social, and personal responsibility and serves as the foundation for all other learning" (p. 23). My parents did educate me each and every day. Unfortunately, I failed to acknowledge the quality and depth of their teaching and naively gave in to the views of many of my psychology professors in the belief that they understood my community better than I did. Additionally, I wanted to tell them that their statements, along with those of my peers, made me feel "othered" (Solorzano & Yosso, 2002) as someone raised outside the normative Western, White, and middle-class cultural narrative.

The impact that Rebeca's course and her mentorship had in my life was the beginning of my transformational resistance (Solorzano & Delgado Bernal, 2001) because in her classroom I found my voice. By writing my *testimonio*, I reframed my personal understanding of my schooling from disenfranchisement to empowerment. Rebeca's unconditional support further helped me feel safe enough to write my story and to eventually share it with others. The *testimonio* assignment, moreover, allowed me to envision graduating from UCSC and pursuing a graduate degree. As I shared my story with her and my peers during our class discussions, for example, I slowly felt myself letting go of the negative schooling experiences that I had internalized for so many years. These negative and emotionally charged experiences were gradually replaced with an educational narrative focused on my resilience as a student. I was able to convert my struggles into victories, and my schooling experiences as an immigrant English language learner (ELL) turned from everlasting hardship to promise.

In addition, by exploring my personal struggles and privileges, I have learned to trust my familial and community values, and to see these as assets that I can use for my own personal and professional work. I have also discovered, as Anzaldúa and Keating (2002) wrote, that "change requires more than words on a page—it takes perseverance, creative ingenuity, and acts of love" (p. 78), which means that we must first be able to love ourselves, as individuals capable of contributing to our own realities. Last, I have realized that my efforts as a social worker should grow from love, which is to care genuinely for the people whom I serve, to see them as they are and not for what they should be.

Rebeca and Natalia: Reflections on *Testimonio* as Critical Pedagogy

We are fortunate to have learned these strategies from other colleagues' transformative experiences of critical pedagogy as mentorship in classrooms of higher education (Cutri, Delgado Bernal, Powell, & Ramirez Wiedeman, 1998; Turner et al., 2012). In reviewing our journeys to educational *testimonios* as critical pedagogy mentorship, we have begun to identify two components of this work that continue to inform our lifework in the academy.

First, we view educational *testimonio* as an intergenerational process that challenges traditional models of mentorship. Despite the pressure to work in solitude in higher education, *testimonio* as critical pedagogy encouraged a co-construction of knowledge and closer working relationship between student and teacher. There is a significant amount of self-disclosure—uncommon in higher education classrooms—that comes with teaching and learning how to write an educational *testimonio*. It was not only the instructor who pushed students to learn, but also the student who created a teaching tool with the presentation of her educational *testimonio*. Natalia taught her instructor *and* her peers different ways of viewing educational trajectories. These opportunities to interrogate our experiences transformed our initial relationship as teacher/student into insider-outsider allies—as Latina women experiencing both marginality and privilege in higher education—helping us better investigate the varied educational trajectories of other students of color.

Second, the process of creating an educational *testimonio* helped us make sense of who we were and who we are becoming through identifying pivotal experiences that have influenced our personal and professional lives. Through reflection and crafting our own narratives alongside those of others, we have been able to reveal silenced tragedies and hopes that we have kept hidden. We have learned that our quest for social justice must begin within ourselves, and has grown through writing and teaching educational *testimonio* as a critical pedagogy. This opportunity to reflect upon our past as we develop new aspirations has provided opportunities to turn challenges into possibilities. These possibilities have included disrupting deficit notions of communities of color in our roles as assistant professor and as a social worker who aspires to the professoriate, in a shared vision of advocating for improved opportunities for youth of color. Like our journeys through and to the academy, our educational *testimonios* are not finished. They have become our working papers—ones we revisit and revise to sustain our journeys.

Implications for the Future

The preparation of an educational *testimonio* is one approach to critical pedagogy that has provided a nontraditional teacher-student mentorship that we did not anticipate finding in the college classroom. We see three policy implications for this work in schools across the country—from preschool to higher education. The first is the incorporation of students' experiences in the curriculum. Central to critical pedagogy is engaging students in the development of self-consciousness (Freire, 1970/1998). As other scholars have noted (Cutri et al., 1998; Turner et al., 2012), the practice of creating affirming learning environments has had lasting effects on student retention and career aspirations. Second, including ethnic and women's studies readings or course requirements has demonstrated growth in students' critical thinking and positive academic and social outcomes (Cabrera, Milem, & Marx, 2012; National Education Association, 2011). Finally, if the academy is serious about widening the pipeline to the professoriate—particularly for students of color—it must invest more in creating opportunities that include teaching and research with first-generation undergraduate students. Our experiences taught us to rethink the boundaries that we often (re)create as instructors and students in higher education—crossing such boundaries is critical for supporting and developing aspirations that include the professoriate.

References

Anzaldúa, G., & Keating, A. (Eds.). (2002). *This bridge we call home: Radical visions for transformation*. New York, NY: Routledge.

Benmayor, R., Torruellas, R. M., & Juarbe, A. L. (1997). Claiming cultural citizenship in East Harlem: *"Si esto puede ayudar a la comunidad mia ..."* In W. V. Flores & R. Benmayor (Eds.), *Latino cultural citizenship: Claiming identity, space, and rights* (pp. 152–209). Boston, MA: Beacon Press.

Burciaga, R. (2007). *Chicana Ph.D. students living nepantla: Educación and aspirations beyond the doctorate* (Unpublished dissertation). University of California, Los Angeles, CA.

Cabrera, N. L., Milem, J. F., & Marx, R. W. (2012). *An empirical analysis of the effects of Mexican American studies participation on student achievement within Tucson Unified School District*. Tucson, AZ: Report to Special Master Dr. Willis D. Hawley on the Tucson Unified School District Desegregation Case.

Clance, P. R., & Imes, S. A. (1978). The impostor phenomenon in high achieving women: Dynamics and therapeutic interventions. *Psychotherapy: Theory, Research and Practice, 15*, 241–247.

Cutri, R. M., Delgado Bernal, D., Powell, A., & Ramirez Wiedeman, C. (1998). "An honorable sisterhood": Developing a critical ethic of care in higher education. *Transformations, 8*(2), 100–117.

de los Reyes, E. (1998). *Syllabus for T128: Education for social and political change.* Cambridge, MA: Harvard Graduate School of Education.

Delgado Bernal, D., Burciaga, R., & Flores Carmona, J. (Eds.). (2012). Chicana/Latina *testimonios*: Mapping the methodological, pedagogical, and political [Special issue]. *Equity and Excellence in Education, 45*(3).

Freire, P. (1970/1998). *Pedagogy of the oppressed* (New rev. 20th-anniversary ed.). New York, NY: Continuum Press.

Gonzalez, N., Moll, L., & Amanti, C. (2005). *Funds of knowledge: Theorizing practice in households, communities, and classrooms*. New York, NY: Routledge.

Gutiérrez, K. D. (2008, April/May/June). Developing a sociocritical literacy in the third space. *Reading Research Quarterly, 43*(2), 148–164.

Gutiérrez y Muhs, G., Flores Niemann, Y., González, C. G., & Harris, A. P. (2012). *Presumed incompetent: The intersections of race and class for women in academia*. Logan, UT: Utah State University Press.

Latina Feminist Group. (2001). *Telling to live: Latina feminist testimonios.* Durham, NC: Duke University Press.

National Education Association. (2011). *The academic and social value of ethnic studies: A research review.* Washington, DC: Sleeter.

Negron-Gonzales, G. (2009). *Hegemony, ideology & oppositional consciousness: Undocumented youth and the personal-political struggle for educational justice.* UC Berkeley Institute for the Study of Societal Issues. Retrieved from http://escholarship.org/uc/item/6z83w4t7

Partnoy, A. (2006). *Cuando vienen matando:* On prepositional shifts and the struggle of testimonial subjects for agency. *PMLA: Publications of the Modern Language Association of America, 121*(5), 1665–1669.

Solorzano, D. G. (1989). Teaching and social change: Reflections on a Freirian approach in a college classroom. *Teaching Sociology, 17*(2), 218–225.

Solorzano, D. G., & Delgado Bernal, D. (2001). Examining transformational resistance through a Critical Race and Latcrit Theory framework: Chicana and Chicano students in an urban context. *Urban Education, 36,* 308–342.

Solorzano, D. G., & Yosso, T. (2002). Critical race methodology: Counter-storytelling as an analytical framework for education research. *Qualitative Inquiry, 8*(1), 23–44.

Turner, C. S. V., Wood, J. L., Montoya, Y. J., Essien-Wood, I. R., Neal, R., Escontrías, G., & Coe, A. (2012). Advancing the next generation of higher education scholars: An examination of one doctoral classroom. *International Journal of Teaching and Learning in Higher Education, 24*(1), 103–112.

Valencia, R. R., & Black, M. S. (2002). "Mexican Americans don't value education!" On the basis of the myth, mythmaking, and debunking. *Journal of Latinos and Education, 1*(2), 81–103.

Valenzuela, A. (1999). Introduction. In *Subtractive schooling* (pp. 3–32). Albany, NY: State University of New York Press.

Yosso, T. J. (2005). Whose culture has capital? A critical race theory discussion of community cultural wealth. *Race Ethnicity and Education, 8*(1), 69–91.

Yosso, T. J. (2006). *Critical race counterstories along the Chicana/Chicano educational pipeline.* New York, NY: Routledge.

Zarate, M. E. (2007). *Understanding Latino parental involvement in education: Perceptions, expectations, and recommendations.* Los Angeles, CA: Tomás Rivera Policy Institute, University of Southern California.

REBECA BURCIAGA is an assistant professor of educational leadership at San José State University, California.

NATALIA CRUZ NAVARRO is currently a post-master's clinical social work trainee in Northern California and holds aspirations to join the professoriate.

This chapter presents an assistant professor's scholarly personal narrative at the precipice of promotion, and reveals how the feral child metaphor might aptly describe many junior professors' experiences as they navigate a path toward tenure. This chronicling of mentorship in sometimes unexpected venues may aid new faculty and those invested in their success in both earning tenure and retaining them in the field.

Of Feral Faculty and Magisterial Mowglis: The Domestication of Junior Faculty

Richard J. Reddick

One of the more fascinating literary and cultural motifs is that of the feral or wild child (a she-wolf raised Romulus and Remus, the founders of the city of Rome; the character Mowgli in Kipling's *The Jungle Book* had an identical upbringing). In fiction, this is characterized ultimately as an advantage, with the feral child avoiding the corrupting societal influences while gaining courage from an upbringing among animals. However, the feral child must endure socialization, an experience of tension and frustration, to become successful within a new societal context. Despite this acclimation, there is a twinge of regret and loss for the feral children who advance to adulthood— they never truly adapt and often return to their roots, only occasionally interacting with civilized society, à la Burroughs's Tarzan and Barrie's Peter Pan.

The feral child of literature is an apt metaphor for my experiences navigating a research-intensive, predominantly White institution (PWI) as a Black male professor. For underrepresented faculty there is a perpetual sense of being the other in PWIs (Stanley, 2006)—and while obtaining degrees and advancing through institutions provide some understanding and access, feeling like an unwelcome guest in a house constructed by and maintained for White, privileged scholars endures. Meanwhile, the socialization process is possible only with the investment of individuals and counter-structures that validate and endorse the feral faculty's existence. My journey from eager naïf to tenured professor illustrates these themes, and I share them here, partly chronicling moments of triumph and disaster buttressed

New Directions for Higher Education, no. 171, Fall 2015 © 2015 Wiley Periodicals, Inc.
Published online in Wiley Online Library (wileyonlinelibrary.com) • DOI: 10.1002/he.20141

43

with theoretical underpinnings on faculty socialization via scholarly personal narrative.

Literature Review

What is the landscape of the academy in 2014, specifically from underrepresented scholars' perspectives? For starters, it is overwhelmingly White. As of fall 2011, 73.4% of faculty members in the United States were White—only slightly more than one quarter of the faculty were of color. Black faculty comprise 6.7%, an uptick from the late 1990s, but hardly approaching equity in a nation that is 13% Black (*Chronicle of Higher Education*, 2013). Other communities of color report similarly paltry levels of representation (e.g., American Indians, 0.5%; Asians, 6.2%; and Hispanics, 5.0%). Unsurprisingly, this underrepresentation has deleterious consequences for faculty of color, and specifically Black faculty. Turner and colleagues (Turner, González, & Wood, 2008) analyzed 20 years of scholarship on the experiences of faculty of color and found numerous factors that positively impacted the workplace for this population: a love for teaching, networking, student diversity, colleagues and allies, political involvement, and supportive leadership. However, adverse factors were greater in number, including undervaluation of their research interests, isolation, bias in hiring, unjust work expectations, a lack of diversity, and a lack of recruitment and retention. Additionally, many factors were presented as both positive and negative, including service, research outlets, and tenure and promotion (Turner et al., 2008).

Researchers have recounted the particularly taxing experiences for Black scholars in PWIs, noting that job satisfaction, representation among tenured faculty, and compensation rank far below the rates for White colleagues (Allen, Epps, Guillory, Suh, & Bonous-Hammarth, 2000). Brayboy (2003), Griffin and Reddick (2011), and Padilla (1994) have focused on the service burden for faculty of color and Black faculty, noting how PWIs exact a "tax" on underrepresented faculty via service and representation regarding campus diversity. While majority faculty are often provided space to initiate research and publications to ensure successful promotion bids, underrepresented faculty deal with pressure from varied constituents, who have levels of expectations for these faculty members, including their engagement with each constituency's needs.

Promotion and tenure can be significant stressors: Concerns about transparency in tenure standards, perception and value of research, and the relative weight of teaching and service compared to research and publication affect underrepresented faculty (Stanley, 2007). The social and instrumental distance between the pathways to success dictated by predominantly White academic norms to the values brought by many scholars of color can be perceived as ferine; the scholar from the underrepresented community is often advised to "civilize" himself or herself to ensure success.

Methodology

How does one "academicize" lived experiences such as those I will relate in this chapter? Scholars are given explicit and implicit messages that autoethnographic scholarship is without depth or rigor. Fortunately, researchers such as Nash (2004) have built a method: *scholarly personal narrative* (SPN), "a 'counter-narrative' to the faceless, de-contextualized research paradigm that has dominated scholarship" (p. vii). Nash further notes that SPN can provide a means for faculty of color to convey experiences, since they "have had to suppress their strong, distinct voices along with their anger, for years in the academy" (p. 2).

While there are commonalities between SPN and autoethnographic methods, SPN "puts the *self* of the scholar front and center … mak[ing] narrative sense of personal experience" (Nash, 2004, p. 18). SPN allows for translating the personal to a larger audience, similar to how scholars of color have leveraged their experiences to challenge and reinterpret established discourses on the academy (see Fries-Britt & Turner Kelly, 2005).

Theoretical Framework

How, then, are feral faculty domesticated? I look to the extant literature on faculty socialization, particularly the work of Austin (2002), for conceptualizations of this process. As Golde (1998) notes, the faculty socialization process begins in graduate school, where a potential faculty member has to first believe that he or she can do the academic work, then commit to graduate student life, and, finally, identify whether he or she belongs in academia; for underrepresented faculty, the final stage may not occur.

Austin (2002) additionally explains that the 21st century presents unique challenges to the faculty socialization process; advancing technology and increasing workloads represent a major transformation of higher education—meaning that the standard for excellence is an ever-elusive target. Increased attention regarding work-life balance in the academy (Reddick, Rochlen, Grasso, Reilly, & Spikes, 2012) is yet another component of socialization. Austin (2002) recommends interventions to facilitate successful socialization, including mentoring, advising, feedback, and greater transparency regarding faculty responsibility.

Cawyer, Simonds, and Davis (2002) present five characteristics that impact faculty socialization: (1) interpersonal bonding (affirming new faculty), (2) social support (emotional care), (3) professional advice (exposing departmental workings), (4) institutional history (knowing the dirty laundry of the organization), and (5) accessibility (new hires feeling they can seek information from senior colleagues). These characteristics aid the civilizing of faculty not privy to dictated mores.

Johnson and Harvey (2002) present one of the few faculty socialization models focused on Black professors, finding three major impediments to

NEW DIRECTIONS FOR HIGHER EDUCATION • DOI: 10.1002/he

faculty socialization: (1) lack of clear communication of institutional values and expectations; (2) lack of transparency from senior faculty, creating barriers to knowledge; and (3) heavy workloads limiting knowledge for promotion and tenure (this finding may be an artifact of the majority of the institutions in the sample being teaching-centered historically Black colleges and universities [HBCUs]). However, one can extrapolate factors that helped and hindered Black faculty socialization—the process where being feral is supplanted by an understanding of a foreign environment's norms and expectations. I can reflect on three aspects of my socialization: *mentoring-at-a-distance*, in which scholars who were invested in my success intervened and supported my trajectory; "*troll models*," colleagues who (in)advertently demonstrated what *not* to do in pursuit of tenure; and *cheerleaders*, who remained optimistic and emphasized the importance of my presence in academia.

Findings

In this section, I provide vignettes from the aforementioned three categories.

Mentoring-at-a-Distance. Mentoring has been traditionally regarded as a close, interpersonal relationship with a senior member of an organization (Kram, 1988). In fact, a defining characteristic of mentorship is proximity; physical distance within developmental relationships leads to the utilization of other forms. My experience speaks to how embracing technology reconceptualizes the meaning of *proximal*. I landed a position at my undergraduate alma mater in my hometown where my family resided, in a department where my presence was welcomed. However, there were concerns unique to my situation and that of my colleague Victor Sáenz, also hired at the same time. For instance, our senior colleagues were tenured decades before, from strong practitioner backgrounds; as researcher-scholars, we found their advice well-intentioned but often inapplicable. Fortunately, the relationships I had established as a graduate student with scholars at other institutions deepened. These "associates" became true mentors, investing time via e-mails, calls, and conference chats. Initially I thought of these as fleeting moments with people I admired, but their influence was far more significant.

Gia is one such mentor-at-a-distance, well known in my subspeciality as a fun-loving but incredibly prolific scholar. I knew Gia socially and had presented a paper with a dear collaborator in a session with her. In the discussion, Gia made points that I had similarly found in some of my work. As I excitedly shared our common findings, Gia asked where the manuscripts had been published. When I replied that they were in an edited volume, she responded, "You really need to get those ideas into peer-reviewed journals!" Initially I was confused; wasn't I supposed to find a broad audience through chapters? Gia's advice, however, was part of the domestication process; scholars need to communicate to multiple constituencies, and the one with the greatest influence on early-career scholars is the peer-review community. One's most significant work should *initially* appear in these venues, while edited volumes are ideal for extensions of this work. As a senior scholar, this seems obvious; nearly a decade ago, I did not understand this aspect of the academy. Gia's gentle but firm admonition alerted me to the fact that I could count on her to give me direct, yet supportive advice.

Over the years, I have consulted Gia over many dilemmas: where to submit manuscripts, navigating the ethics of the publication process, and how to graciously decline opportunities to publish chapters with prominent scholars. I know Gia does this for a multitude of junior scholars, but she is gifted in making her mentees feel as if she is exclusively focused on their careers. I use the term *mentoring magnet* to describe scholars such as Gia, who despite distance and an incredibly active research agenda find time to invest in a number of junior scholars.

Another mentoring magnet who served as a mentor-at-a-distance is Magdalena, whose work I voraciously read during my dissertation writing. I had the opportunity to meet Magdalena a few times, but thought that I was just one of the faces she politely spoke to on the conference circuit. During my first year as a faculty member, I learned she was paying closer attention than I had thought. In an e-mail exchange about a conference symposium mix-up, she added this note:

> I met some doctoral students who mentioned you at a conference [related to your research agenda] recently. They had many positive things to say about you and your work. Thought you would like to know.

It may seem like a minor pat on the back, but for a junior professor in an eternal state of self-doubt, hearing a senior scholar compliment my work and connection to students was incredibly validating. I returned to this e-mail after receiving rejections from journal editors, using it as motivation—*a prominent, well-published scholar in my field thinks highly of my work; sooner or later one of these manuscripts will get accepted!*

Years on, I have made the most of the brief time I spend face-to-face with Magdalena, but our correspondence via e-mail is lengthy and meaningful. When I was in the editing stage of a manuscript submitted to a prestigious journal, Magdalena was one of the first to ask about its status so that she could cite it in her work. Magdalena has opened networks, and, through her scholarship and mentorship, has pioneered a path validating a place for scholars such as myself who bring multiple identities in contrast to the dominant population at many PWIs.

There are many examples of mentoring-at-a-distance in my journey. Jamal, who included me in numerous projects as I started in the professoriate, although he was not in my exact subspecialty; Kwame, who suggested I investigate family-friendly policies such as the clock stoppage I ultimately employed when my daughter was born prematurely; and Jabari, whom I would see at the annual conference and who would connect me to other scholars in the field via his expansive network. Many of these mentors worked across various axes of identity to provide metaphorical shelter from the storm of achieving tenure at a research-intensive institution.

"Troll Models."   Young scholars look to peers and senior colleagues for guidance; I was no exception. However, as instructive as those colleagues were who showed me how to best utilize my skills, I may have learned as much from those who navigated the academy incongruent to my values. I use the term *troll models* to describe these scholars. It is only fair to note that many of these scholars simply chose a different pathway than mine and that this nomenclature is somewhat provocative. Nevertheless, from these examples I realized I had to strive for another direction in the academy. A good colleague of mine in the policy world, Vernon, demonstrated what a troll model could be. After a visit, I asked, "Why did you choose to not join the professoriate? You love research, and you're an excellent teacher—this is the perfect life for you." Vernon recounted a discussion he'd had with Bill, a senior scholar we both knew. After Bill had extolled the benefits of an academic career to Vernon at a cookout, Vernon found himself sitting next to Bill's teenaged son. Vernon asked Bill's son what he thought of his dad's career, and the son responded: "I guess it's great, especially now that he's well established in his field. I see a lot more of him now. When I was younger, he was always traveling. I guess now I'm kind of getting to know my dad for the first time."

Vernon's story struck me. My son, Karl, was born in October during my first year as a professor, and I remember responding to e-mails with a sleeping infant on my chest (not easy, but possible). My spouse pointed out to me that it *might* work better if I was able to focus on parenting when I was at home; I shamefully agreed. Since then, I think I've done a much better job of balancing work and family. I carve out time to take Karl to karate class, and I've been at virtually every school event for both him and my daughter, Katherine. From my own research, I know that junior faculty men still grapple with utilizing family-friendly policies at work. However, I have endeavored to be as present as I can be in my family's lives. I am relieved to have earned tenure, because it does suggest that the promotion process does have some regard for the soul as well as the mind.

I am not perfect, and occasionally disappear to check e-mails or finish a manuscript. The example of senior scholars a generation or two before me has instructed me to prioritize some aspects of my life differently. I am fully aware that someone with different priorities may take advantage of opportunities that I would bypass. I am at peace with this understanding—and I will admit, as the children get older, there's a little more freedom in my schedule.

I have encountered other troll models. There were scholars who advised me to "just say no" (the Nancy Reagan mantra) to service or connecting with the community, without realizing that I research and teach in the community from whence I came; I am a homecoming faculty member of color (Reddick & Sáenz, 2012). Wiser advisors urged me to integrate service, teaching, and research—advice that acknowledged my admiration for those in the community who made it possible for me to become a professor. My troll model examples work for *some* in academia; there are multiple ways for an academic life. Fortunately, I had counterexamples to the paths I found worrisome.

Cheerleaders.   I discussed the impact of mentors-at-a-distance earlier; cheerleaders are a little different. These supporters are not always faculty colleagues; for me, they are advisees, students, friends, or professional colleagues in other fields. They are there to support the team, regardless of what the scoreboard reads. I recall students' e-mails precisely when I receive a disappointing article review or an unsuccessful grant proposal review. This e-mail arrived about a month into fatherhood, when I was unsure whether I was wearing clean clothes or shaving on a daily basis:

> Thank you for bringing so much additional material to your lectures each week. As a feminist it is *extremely* difficult to sit through readings and lectures that seem to revolve around the role men (particularly Anglo men) have played in the world; your efforts to recognize the relevant efforts of both female and minority individuals in the context of higher education did not go unnoticed and were much appreciated. I wish you the best in your academic career here at UT!

Messages of this ilk are the lifeblood of the day-to-day academic grind. Previously, as a teacher, I remember a mentor urging me to greet every child with a smile and hello, "because you might be the only person to do it that day." Similarly, one of these "cheers" can be one of the few positive moments in a day festooned with failure. The nature of rigor and competition necessitates being on the losing end at times; encouragement from cheerleaders keeps one in the game.

The high service loads for scholars of color at PWIs leads to what I term "associate assistanthood." Many of the obligations that traditionally are the domain of senior faculty (chairing departmental committees, chairing dissertations, and directing degree programs) can fall into the hands of assistant professors. This is not a complaint; the reality of working in a small department is that these things must be done, and senior colleagues bear a greater share of the burden. Cheerleaders mediate the load in many ways: A regular discussion among students in my department was how to access new faculty in a nonburdensome manner. Many advanced students served as informal gatekeepers, redirecting students to senior faculty or assisting junior colleagues with concerns to protect my time. I was awestruck when one advisee shared how she had taught a peer about conference proposals, "because *you* don't need to be spending your time worrying about that." I also had the support of emeritus faculty, who agreed to serve on committees or guest lecture in courses. Just as cheerleaders will build a pyramid by serving as the base while allowing a teammate to climb to the apex, these advisees, friends, and professional and emeritus colleagues allowed me to stand on the shoulders of giants (though they are too humble to see themselves as such). In my mind, they are giants in generosity and kindness.

Discussion and Conclusion

I have stretched the feral metaphor to the limit in this narrative; however, it aptly conveys an enlightening socialization process that I have experienced. Despite the chasm that separates my being from the predominantly White academy, I am slowly finding support externally and internally that validates my place, as Austin (2002) and Golde (1998) note within the final stage of graduate student development. Pre-tenure, I felt I had been granted the opportunity to sink or swim; I have emerged afloat.

The ever-evolving role of the faculty has made mentors-at-a-distance increasingly important; they have demonstrated a humane path toward the life of the mind. Mentors-at-a-distance and cheerleaders interpersonally affirmed my presence in the field, demonstrating care for my entire being while revealing the inner workings of the academy. I was armored with knowledge to supplement on-campus mentors, who informed me of the institution-specific realities of academia, corresponding to conceptualizations of faculty socialization (Cawyer et al., 2002; Miller, 1995). Furthermore, through knowledge of the field at large and experiences at peer institutions, mentors-at-a-distance were often more forthcoming about likely tenure expectations than local senior colleagues, in line with Johnson and Harvey's (2002) findings about socialization for Black faculty. Conversely, troll models have helped me understand the consequences of certain choices; I am better equipped to make decisions knowing potential outcomes.

So having reached tenure, am I fully domesticated? *No!* I revel in the fact that my journey has been somewhat out of sync with the prevailing pathways of socialization, though I benefited from support mechanisms through different sources. I still embrace emblematic methodologies and theories outside of the academy—such as this chapter. Simultaneously, I have been accultured to my field's tenets. In conversation with colleagues of color at PWIs, I have found that this is a commonly held sentiment. For feral faculty, occupying this middle space is our ultimate destination, with the flickers of wildness peeking through the veneer of academic civilization. It is becoming a more comfortable space, as I echo the sentiments of Voltaire: "Froth at the top, dregs at bottom, but the middle excellent."

References

Allen, W. R., Epps, E. G., Guillory, E. A., Suh, S. A., & Bonous-Hammarth, M. (2000). The Black academic: Faculty status among African Americans in U.S. higher education. *Journal of Negro Education, 69*(1–2), 112–127.

Austin, A. E. (2002). Preparing the next generation of faculty: Graduate school as socialization to the academic career. *Journal of Higher Education, 73*(1), 94–122.

Brayboy, B. M. J. (2003). The implementation of diversity in predominantly White colleges and universities. *Journal of Black Studies, 34*(1), 72–86.

Cawyer, C. S., Simonds, C., & Davis, S. (2002). Mentoring to facilitate socialization: The case of the new faculty member. *International Journal of Qualitative Studies in Education, 15*(2), 225–242.

Chronicle of Higher Education. (2013). *Race and ethnicity of college administrators, faculty, and staff, fall 2011* [Table]. Retrieved from http://chronicle.com/article/RaceEthnicity-of-College/140173/

Fries-Britt, S. L., & Turner Kelly, B. (2005). Retaining each other: Narratives of two African American women in the academy. *Urban Review, 37*(3), 221–242.

Golde, C. M. (1998). Beginning graduate school: Examining first-year doctoral attrition. In M. S. Anderson (Ed.), *New Directions for Higher Education: No. 101. The experience of being in graduate school: An exploration* (pp. 55–64). San Francisco, CA: Jossey-Bass.

Griffin, K. A., & Reddick, R. J. (2011). Surveillance and sacrifice: Gender differences in the mentoring patterns of Black professors at predominantly White research universities. *American Educational Research Journal, 48*(5), 1032–1057.

Johnson, B. J., & Harvey, W. B. (2002). The socialization of Black college faculty: Implications for policy and practice. *Review of Higher Education, 25*(3), 297–314.

Kram, K. E. (1988). *Mentoring at work: Developmental relationships in organizational life.* Lanham, MD: University Press of America.

Miller, K. (1995). *Organizational communication: Approaches and processes.* Belmont, CA: Wadsworth.

Nash, R. J. (2004). *Liberating scholarly narrative: The power of personal narrative.* New York, NY: Teachers College Press.

Padilla, A. M. (1994). Ethnic minority scholars, research, and mentoring: Current and future issues. *Educational Researcher, 23*(4), 24–27.

Reddick, R. J., Rochlen, A. B., Grasso, J. R., Reilly, E. R., & Spikes, D. R. (2012). Academic fathers pursuing tenure: A qualitative study of work-family conflict, coping strategies, and departmental culture. *Psychology of Men & Masculinity, 13*(1), 1–15.

Reddick, R. J., & Sáenz, V. B. (2012). Coming home: *Hermanos académicos* reflect on paths and present realities at their home institution. *Harvard Educational Review, 82*(3), 353–380.

Stanley, C. A. (2006). Coloring the academic landscape: Faculty of color breaking the silence in predominantly White colleges and universities. *American Educational Research Journal, 43*(4), 701–736.

Stanley, C. A. (2007). When counter narratives meet master narratives in the journal editorial review process. *Educational Researcher, 36*(1), 14–24.

Turner, C. S. V., González, J. C., & Wood, J. L. (2008). Faculty of color in academe: What 20 years of literature tells us. *Journal of Diversity in Higher Education, 1*(3), 139–168.

RICHARD J. REDDICK is an associate professor of higher education with appointments in the Warfield Center for African and African American Studies, the Department of African and African Diaspora Studies, and the Division of Diversity and Community Engagement at the University of Texas–Austin. He also serves as assistant director of the Plan II Honors Program.

6

This chapter outlines the psychosocial aspects of mentoring that help women combat the barriers they commonly face in science, technology, engineering, and mathematics (STEM). The authors describe the CareerWISE online resilience training and how it can address the shortage of effective mentors and role models who have been shown to increase the persistence of women in STEM fields.

Providing the Psychosocial Benefits of Mentoring to Women in STEM: *Career*WISE as an Online Solution

Amy E. Dawson, Bianca L. Bernstein, Jennifer M. Bekki

Effective mentoring, recognized to be an important component in the academic and professional development of women and minorities, may well be one of the most critical elements in the progression of women toward advanced degrees in science, technology, engineering, and mathematics (STEM) fields. In STEM, where, despite progress, the proportion of doctorates awarded to women still hovers around 20% in computer science, physics, and engineering (National Science Board, 2014), and the attrition of enrolled women from doctoral programs exceeds that of men by as much as 9% (Council of Graduate Schools, 2008), the promise of purposive mentoring demands attention.

Evidence is accumulating that women's persistence in the sciences and engineering, a matter of urgent national concern (National Academy of Sciences, National Academy of Engineering, and Institute of Medicine, 2007), is directly linked to the availability of a strong mentor (Preston, 2004). For example, in Preston's (2004) study, six out of seven women identified a lack of guidance and support as a reason for their decision to leave science. Moreover, women who received mentoring during graduate school completed their graduate programs at a rate of 100%, compared to 60% among women who did not receive mentoring during their graduate years (Preston, 2004). That mentoring is linked to an increase in the probability of completing a program in STEM and that lack of guidance is associated with a greater risk

---

This material is based on work supported by the National Science Foundation under Grant Numbers 0634519 and 0910384.

New Directions for Higher Education, no. 171, Fall 2015 © 2015 Wiley Periodicals, Inc.
Published online in Wiley Online Library (wileyonlinelibrary.com) • DOI: 10.1002/he.20142

of attrition suggest that the essential elements of effective mentoring and how these can be delivered must be clearly understood.

In this chapter, we point to the barriers that women face in STEM fields and describe the elements of mentoring that address them. We discuss the challenges of developing mentoring relationships, and highlight the growing use of alternative forms of mentoring. We conclude by introducing the *Career*WISE online resource (https://careerwise.asu.edu) as a free and internationally available alternative to in-person mentoring, highlighting how its key learning goals map to some of the known positive effects of mentoring.

The Obstacle Course for Women in STEM

Women are leaving STEM fields due not to a deficit in academic preparation, ability, or talent (Seymour & Hewitt, 1994; Sonnert & Holton, 1995), but rather to a drop in confidence that is triggered by a range of experiences along the STEM pathway. Environmental obstacles include problematic advising and a severely competitive academic environment that runs counter to women's preferences for collaboration (Bernstein & Russo, 2008). In contrast to men who report becoming bored or disappointed in their program (Seymour & Hewitt, 1994), some women experience significant discouragement and isolation in a chilly climate that includes few role models and mentors, a dearth of female peers, intimidation, and implicit or overt bias against women. The feelings of not belonging, isolation, and a shortage of mentoring appear to be instrumental in women's decisions to leave science (Fabert, Cabay, Rivers, Smith, & Bernstein, 2011; Preston, 2004; Rayman & Brett, 1995; Rosser, 2004). In a study of women who left doctoral programs in STEM fields, participants described an erosion of confidence as advisors and sometimes partners actively discouraged or more frequently failed to encourage them to pursue their goals and to persist (Fabert & Bernstein, 2009). Substantial efforts have been made over time to improve the academic climates for women in STEM fields (e.g., the AD-VANCE projects supported by the National Science Foundation), but the individual instances and cumulative effects of discouragement and declining confidence are what remain to be addressed in order to support talented women's persistence in STEM fields.

The perceived difficulty in balancing a demanding career and a fulfilling family life is identified by some women as a significant obstruction to their career in science (Bernstein & Russo, 2007; Ferriman, Lubinski, & Benbow, 2009; Rosser, 2004). In one study, 65% of both male and female doctoral students surveyed reported that they planned to have children; however, 46% of women compared to 21% of men cited issues related to children as a reason for shifting their career goal away from an academic research career (Mason, Goulden, & Frasch, 2009). Among graduate students in departments where female faculty frequently had children, 46% tended to view tenure-track faculty positions as family friendly; in comparison, only

12% of students in departments where very few female professors had children viewed an academic career as family friendly (Mason et al., 2009). The data highlight the power of female role models, especially in high-intensity professions, who demonstrate the possibilities and potentials for successfully combining a family and career. Given the noted lack of female faculty in STEM fields, it is critical to identify alternative means to provide support and role modeling to women who plan to pursue both professional and family formation goals.

The Psychological Processes and Outcomes of Effective Mentoring

The positive effects of mentoring, especially when conflated with advising, include increased research productivity and professional skills of the mentee (Green, 1991; Lyons, Scroggins, & Rule, 1990; Paglis, Green, & Bauer, 2006; Schlosser, Lyons, Talleyrand, Kim, & Johnson, 2011). In this regard, the instrumental function of mentoring can be described as guidance through the technicalities of the academic program, the provision of academic knowledge support, and instruction and intellectual provocation by the mentor to the mentee (Nora & Crisp, 2007; Primé, Bernstein, Wilkins, & Bekki, 2014). Effective mentoring and advising can also assist mentees in strengthening research self-efficacy, better assessing their own strengths and weaknesses, setting academic and career goals, and recognizing professional development opportunities (Paglis et al., 2006).

For women in STEM, however, an equally critical aspect of mentoring is providing the psychosocial support to counter the elevated stress and discouragement and the falling confidence that some experience. The psychosocial component entails encouragement, emotional support, mutual understanding, and guidance on a more personal level (George & Neale, 2006; Nora & Crisp, 2007; Primé et al., 2014). Women appreciate mentors who are aware of the differential experiences of men and women in STEM fields, and who can understand their unique challenges (Bernstein, Jacobson, & Russo, 2010; Etzkowitz, Kemelgor, & Uzzi, 2000). Role modeling and counsel, along with friendship and acceptance, appear to be important elements of psychosocial mentoring for women as well (Baranik, Roling, & Eby, 2010; Rayman & Brett, 1995).

Psychosocial support offered by mentors moderates the effect of environmental barriers on psychological outcomes (Bernstein & Russo, 2008). This phenomenon can best be understood within the context of social support—that is, encouragement that buffers a sense of isolation and protects against stress-induced mood disorders and physical symptoms (Southwick, Vythilingam, & Charney, 2005). Importantly, psychosocial support contributes to stress resilience and career satisfaction by increasing positivity, cognitive flexibility, sense of meaning, empowerment, and active coping strategies.

Arguably, the most potent outcomes of psychosocial support offered by effective mentors are increased self-efficacy (i.e., stronger confidence about performing in a specific domain such as a science or engineering field) and coping efficacy (i.e., a mentee's confidence in her ability to navigate the stressors she experiences along the STEM pathway). Role models and mentors who provide psychosocial support can help mentees better cope with biases and misunderstandings, counter the effects of unpleasant working environments, construct a dual commitment to career and family, and reduce burnout and exhaustion by demonstrating effective coping strategies and providing new or different perspectives while remaining sensitive to a woman's experience of marginalization and doubt (Dean & Simpson, 2013; Van Emmerik, 2004). Self-efficacy and coping efficacy are thought to predict women's satisfaction with degree programs and ultimately persistence in STEM, reinforcing the vital role that role models and mentors can play (Bernstein & Russo, 2008).

Challenges to Mentoring Relationships

Mentoring is associated with degree completion and career advancement for women and minorities. Yet, in a Nettles and Millett (2006) study, 31% of graduate students reported having no mentoring at all. Among those graduate students who did report having a mentor and research assistantships, men showed a significant advantage over women in the number of paper presentations and published research articles. Nettles and Millett point to women's lower ratings of their interactions with faculty as a possible explanation for the gender differences in productivity.

Indeed, even when instrumental advising and mentoring may be provided, women's access to the psychosocial aspects of mentoring in STEM fields is rare. Not surprisingly, in fields such as education, nursing, and psychology, attention to support and encouragement is linked to the nature of the helping professions and the large number of women. In the physical science and engineering fields, by contrast, women students are far outnumbered by men, there may be no or few female faculty members, and the masculine environment is often characterized by an emphasis on productivity and competitive advantage, individualism, objectivity, and unexamined gender bias and stereotyping. In these environments, women students report disrespectful treatment of their ideas, embedded hints that they don't belong, patronizing and otherwise uncomfortable interactions, and unsatisfactory support for their personal commitments (Gunter & Stambach, 2005; Noy & Ray, 2012; Ulku-Steiner, Kurtz-Costes, & Kinlaw, 2000).

Institutional efforts to establish mentoring programs are important but are unlikely to remedy, in the short term or even in the longer term, the scarcity of the psychosocial mentoring that particularly benefits women. Clearly, there is need to change the traditional view of formal, dyadic relationships with mentors, and creative approaches to psychosocial components of mentoring are warranted.

*Career*WISE: Psychosocial Mentoring Available Online

Recent years have shown inroads in showcasing role models and mentoring relationships through written and recorded mechanisms. Mentoring relationships through correspondence are gaining in popularity and have been found to be advantageous, particularly for women and minorities who tend to have difficulty finding mentors (Knouse, 2001; Muller & Barsion, 2003). Computer-mediated models are available for matching protégés with mentors in different work sectors such as athletic coaching, public relations, and student teaching (Ensher, Heun, & Blanchard, 2003). What all of these mentoring sites have in common is a departure from the traditional dyadic and colocated form of mentoring and a movement toward mentoring as expanding a supportive network (Ensher et al., 2003).

*Career*WISE (http://careerwise.asu.edu) is a unique and empirically validated approach to mentoring that is freely offered online and is designed to provide some of the psychosocial functions of support and guidance that so many women in STEM fields have been missing (Bernstein, 2011). The *Career*WISE curriculum, based on an extensive program of research tracing the psychological precursors of women's choices either to persist in or to leave science and engineering programs and careers, is crafted to deliberately strengthen resilience, problem-solving, and coping skills (Bernstein, 2011). The *Career*WISE program of psychological education provides instruction, practice, and vicarious role models, customized for women in STEM fields, in personal and interpersonal skills for overcoming discouragers, managing barriers, and expanding supports to fulfill personal and professional ambitions. The framework extends the problem-solving method that scientists and engineers use for technical problems to the personal and interpersonal issues associated with advancement in academic arenas.

The *Career*WISE website features more than 50 educational modules, such as Build on Your Strengths, Self-Talk, Your Personality and Preferences, Consider Other Perspectives, Stereotype Threat, Recognize Sexism, and Family-Friendly Policies, which focus on the personal and environmental contributors to distress and resilience and provide instruction on how to handle the sometimes inhospitable environments that women in STEM fields experience (Bekki, Smith, Bernstein, & Harrison, 2013; Bernstein, 2011). The modules rely heavily on psychological research and include a selection of supporting references along with embedded self-tests.

HerStories are an innovative feature of *Career*WISE intended to showcase role models that are otherwise unavailable to women in STEM fields. Specifically, the *Career*WISE resilience training offers almost 200 video clips from interviews with successful women in STEM fields. STEM professionals detail their experiences in graduate school and early professional life, thereby normalizing many of the difficulties women graduate students believe are unique to them. Conceptualized as coping models and opportunities for vicarious learning, the HerStory clips reveal coping strategies and advice for common experiences such as managing multiple roles of scientist and mother, overcoming self-doubt, and dealing with sexist interactions.

A new portion of the website devoted solely to communication and how to use it effectively to solve problems and overcome barriers has recently been added to the site (Primé et al., 2013). Some of the new communication curriculum includes modules such as Active Listening, Receiving and Responding to Feedback, and Conflict Management, all designed to help students master fundamental communication skills and use them to promote themselves professionally and get what they want out of their education and career (Primé et al., 2013).

Further, three interactive, multimedia simulations with live actors were developed as a supplement to the text of the communication curriculum to help students practice what they learn. Each of the simulations reinforces a specific set of communication skills (subsumed under Active Listening, Expressing Yourself, or Receiving and Responding to Feedback), and is tied to scenarios that our research has shown to be problematic for women in the sciences and engineering fields (difficulties with getting needed help from advisors, dealing assertively with conflicting commitments to a partner and research, and managing critical feedback from a research supervisor that is tinged with gender bias).

Each video-based simulation is similar to a "Choose Your Own Adventure" model and provides several opportunities for users to decide how to respond. After each video clip from a live-action scenario, the user chooses one of three options; one alternative is neutral, another represents the option that is most likely to result in a successful outcome, and a third is not at all likely to result in a successful outcome (Bernstein, Bekki, Harrison, & Wilkins, 2014). Following a participant's selection, a narrator provides feedback and another video shows how the chosen response influences the progression of the interpersonal exchange (Primé et al., 2013). The cycle of video, response selection, narrator feedback, and subsequent interaction continues until the correct choices are made (Bernstein et al., 2014).

Three key studies have demonstrated the effectiveness of the *Career*WISE program in leading to targeted knowledge and skills. A randomized controlled trial (RCT) with 133 female doctoral students in STEM fields assigned to either a treatment group or a wait-list control demonstrated that even a small amount of exposure to the original *Career*WISE resource significantly increased skill measures of problem solving, resilience, and coping efficacy, all of which are linked to persistence

(Bekki et al., 2013). Furthermore, in a recent exploratory study, graduate women in STEM at risk of attrition (due to a lack of advisor support and guidance) scored significantly higher on problem-solving knowledge and measures of variables associated with persistence after interacting with the CareerWISE resource than those at-risk participants who were not exposed to CareerWISE (Dawson, Bernstein, & Bekki, 2013). In the third study, 301 female doctoral students in STEM were assigned to one of three treatment conditions: three hours of interaction with the text-based communication skills curriculum, three hours of access to the text-based communication curriculum plus the interactive simulations, or a wait-list control. Preliminary analyses of the data suggest that participants in the two treatment groups scored significantly higher than the wait-list control participants on the target measures of communication knowledge and skills, as well as on communication coping efficacy.

Conclusion

Women in STEM fields commonly face a range of barriers in their progression toward degree completion and careers in STEM. Of primary concern is that women have limited access to advisors and mentors who can provide the psychosocial aspects of mentoring that have been shown to bolster success and persistence, buffer discouragement, and attenuate decisions to leave science. CareerWISE is described as an effective online alternative or supplement to traditional in-vivo mentoring. The CareerWISE program aims to increase women's resilience, problem-solving, coping, and communication skills. In addition to comprehensive text-based instruction, unique features include HerStories (i.e., clips from interviews with STEM professionals who serve as role and coping models for students in male-dominated environments), and a set of interactive simulations that provide practice in communicating in difficult situations common to female students in STEM fields. The findings of three studies lend empirical support to the possibility that the psychosocial support and resilience training offered by CareerWISE can lessen the risks associated with a range of barriers and unwelcoming environments encountered by women in STEM. Our hope is that women in STEM will obtain the skills, resources, and encouragement they need to combat discouragement and to persist in STEM education, occupations, and careers.

References

Baranik, L. E., Roling, E. A., & Eby, L. T. (2010). Why does mentoring work? The role of perceived organizational support. *Journal of Vocational Behavior, 76*(3), 366–373.

Bekki, J. M., Smith, M. L., Bernstein, B. L., & Harrison, C. J. (2013). Effects of an online personal resilience training program for women in STEM doctoral programs. *Journal of Women and Minorities in Science and Engineering, 19*(1), 17–35.

Bernstein, B. L. (2011). Managing barriers and building supports in science and engineering doctoral programs: Conceptual underpinnings for a new online training program for women. *Journal of Women and Minorities in Science and Engineering, 17*(1), 29–50.

Bernstein, B. L., Bekki, J. M., Harrison, C. J., & Wilkins, K. G. (2014). *Analysis of instructional support elements for an online, educational simulation on active listening.* Manuscript submitted for publication.

Bernstein, B. L., Jacobson, R., & Russo, N. F. (2010). Mentoring women in context: Focus on science, technology, engineering, and mathematics fields. In C. A. Rayburn, F. L. Denmark, M. E. Reuder, & A. M. Austria (Eds.), *A handbook for women mentors: Transcending barriers of stereotype, race, and ethnicity* (pp. 43–64). Westport, CT: Praeger Press.

Bernstein, B. L., & Russo, N. F. (2007). Career paths and family in the academy: Progress and challenges. In M. A. Paludi & P. E. Neidermeyer (Eds.), *Work, life, and family imbalance: How to level the playing field* (pp. 89–119). Westport, CT: Praeger Press.

Bernstein, B. L., & Russo, N. F. (2008). Explaining too few women in academic science and engineering careers: A psychosocial perspective. In M. Paludi (Series Ed.), *The psychology of women at work: Challenges and solutions for our female workforce: Vol. 2. Obstacles and the identity juggle* (pp. 1–33). Westport, CT: Praeger Press.

Council of Graduate Schools. (2008). *Ph.D. completion and attrition: Analysis of baseline demographic data from the Ph.D. completion project.* Washington, DC: Author.

Dawson, A. E., Bernstein, B. L., & Bekki, J. M. (2013). *Alternative mentoring for graduate women in STEM at risk of attrition: A preliminary study.* Unpublished manuscript.

Dean, D. J., & Simpson, C. L. (2013). Mentoring postdoctoral women from an institutional perspective. In K. F. Ehm & C. J. Phillips (Eds.), *From PhD to professoriate: The role of the institution in fostering the advancement of postdoc women* (pp. 59–62). Washington, DC: National Postdoctoral Association.

Ensher, E. A., Heun, C., & Blanchard, A. (2003). Online mentoring and computer-mediated communication: New directions in research. *Journal of Vocational Behavior, 63,* 264–288.

Etzkowitz, H., Kemelgor, C., & Uzzi, B. (2000). *Athena unbound: The advancement of women in science and technology.* Cambridge, UK: Cambridge University Press.

Fabert, N., & Bernstein, B. L. (2009, August). *Women's attrition from STEM doctoral programs: Reflections from non-completers.* Paper presented at the meeting of the American Psychological Association, Toronto, Canada.

Fabert, N., Cabay, M., Rivers, M., Smith, M. L., & Bernstein, B. L. (2011). Exaggerating the typical and stereotyping the differences: Isolation experienced by women in STEM doctoral programs. *Proceedings of the American Society for Engineering Education* (AC 2011-704).

Ferriman, K., Lubinski, D., & Benbow, C. P. (2009). Work preferences, life values, and personal views of top math/science graduate students and the profoundly gifted: Developmental changes and gender differences during emerging adulthood and parenthood. *Journal of Personality and Social Psychology, 97*(3), 517–532.

George, Y. S., & Neale, D. (2006). *Report from study group meetings to develop a research and action agenda on STEM career and workforce mentoring.* Retrieved from http://ehrweb.aaas.org/sciMentoring/MentoringReport.pdf

Green, S. G. (1991). Professional entry and the adviser relationship: Socialization, commitment, and productivity. *Group and Organization Studies, 16*(4), 387–407.

Gunter, R., & Stambach, A. (2005). Differences in men and women scientists' perceptions of workplace climate. *Journal of Women and Minorities in Science and Engineering, 11*(1), 97–116.

Knouse, S. B. (2001). Virtual mentors: Mentoring on the Internet. *Journal of Employment Counseling, 38*(4), 162–169.

Lyons, W., Scroggins, D., & Rule, P. B. (1990). The mentor in graduate education. *Studies in Higher Education, 15*(3), 277–285.

Mason, M. A., Goulden, M., & Frasch, K. (2009). Why graduate students reject the fast track. *Academe, 95*(1), 11–16.

Muller, C. B., & Barsion, S. J. (2003). Assessment of a large-scale e-mentoring network for women in engineering and science: Just how good is MentorNet? *Proceedings of the Women in Engineering Program Advocates Network, Chicago, Illinois* (pp. 1–6).

National Academy of Sciences, National Academy of Engineering, and Institute of Medicine. (2007). *Beyond bias and barriers: Fulfilling the potential of women in academic science and engineering.* Washington, DC: National Academies Press.

National Science Board. (2014). *Science and engineering indicators 2014* (NSB 14-01). Arlington, VA: National Science Foundation.

Nettles, M. T., & Millett, C. M. (2006). *Three magic letters: Getting to Ph.D.* Baltimore, MD: Johns Hopkins University Press.

Nora, A., & Crisp, G. (2007). Mentoring students: Conceptualizing and validating the multi-dimensions of a support system. *Journal of College Student Retention: Research, Theory and Practice, 9*(3), 337–356.

Noy, S., & Ray, R. (2012). Graduate students' perceptions of their advisors: Is there systematic disadvantage in mentorship? *Journal of Higher Education, 83*(6), 876–914.

Paglis, L. L., Green, S. G., & Bauer, T. N. (2006). Does adviser mentoring add value? A longitudinal study of mentoring and doctoral student outcomes. *Research in Higher Education, 47*(4), 451–476.

Preston, A. E. (2004). *Leaving science: Occupational exit from science careers.* New York, NY: Russell Sage Foundation.

Primé, D., Bernstein, B. L., Way, A., Hita, L., Liddell, T., Sarma, A., & Bekki, J. M. (2013). Development of an Internet-delivered communication curriculum for graduate women in STEM. *Proceedings of the American Society of Engineering Education (ASEE)* (paper ID # 7544).

Primé, D. R., Bernstein, B. L., Wilkins, K. G., & Bekki, J. M. (2014). Measuring the advising alliance for female graduate students in science and engineering: An emerging structure. *Journal of Career Assessment, 22*(1), 1–15.

Rayman, P., & Brett, B. (1995). Women science majors: What makes a difference in persistence after graduation? *Journal of Higher Education, 66*(4), 388–414.

Rosser, S. V. (2004). *The science glass ceiling: Academic women scientists and the struggle to succeed.* New York, NY: Routledge.

Schlosser, L. Z., Lyons, H. Z., Talleyrand, R. M., Kim, B. S., & Johnson, W. B. (2011). Advisor-advisee relationships in graduate training programs. *Journal of Career Development, 38*(1), 3–18.

Seymour, E., & Hewitt, N. M. (1994). *Talking about leaving: Factors contributing to high attrition rates among science, mathematics, and engineering undergraduate majors.* Boulder: University of Colorado.

Sonnert, G., & Holton, G. J. (1995). *Who succeeds in science? The gender dimension.* New Brunswick, NJ: Rutgers University Press.

Southwick, S. M., Vythilingam, M., & Charney, D. S. (2005). The psychobiology of depression and resilience to stress: Implications for prevention and treatment. *Annual Review of Clinical Psychology, 1*, 255–291.

Ulku-Steiner, B., Kurtz-Costes, B., & Kinlaw, C. R. (2000). Doctoral student experiences in gender-balanced and male-dominated graduate programs. *Journal of Educational Psychology, 92*(2), 296–307.

Van Emmerik, H. (2004). For better and for worse: Adverse working conditions and the beneficial effects of mentoring. *Career Development International, 9*(4), 358–373.

AMY E. DAWSON *is a doctoral student in counseling psychology in the College of Letters and Sciences at Arizona State University.*

BIANCA L. BERNSTEIN *is professor of counseling and counseling psychology in the College of Letters and Sciences at Arizona State University.*

JENNIFER M. BEKKI *is an associate professor in The Polytechnic School within the Fulton Schools of Engineering at Arizona State University.*

NEW DIRECTIONS FOR HIGHER EDUCATION • DOI: 10.1002/he

7

This chapter describes how sustained mentoring together with rigorous collaborative learning and community building contributed to successful mathematical research and individual growth in the Applied Mathematical Sciences Summer Institute (AMSSI), a program that focused on women, underrepresented minorities, and individuals from small teaching institutions who might not have had the opportunity to do research otherwise. The collective learning and developmental experiences of AMSSI's cofounders as students, teaching assistants, and faculty in other research programs, together with their humble upbringings and cultural histories, are what define the unique structure and mentoring blueprint of AMSSI.

Transforming the Undergraduate Research Experience Through Sustained Mentoring: Creating a Strong Support Network and a Collaborative Learning Environment

Erika T. Camacho, Raquell M. Holmes, Stephen A. Wirkus

Our work addresses the obstacle to diversifying the professoriate that is created by the societal structure of the United States that has yet to move poor, working-class students into the mainstream (Fulani, 2013). Although the largest number of people living in poverty are White (9.5% of the White population), greater percentages of African American (27.6%) and Hispanic (25.3%) populations are in poverty (U.S. Census Bureau, 2011). Why is this relevant to a chapter on mentoring in higher education? As Fulani (1984) showed in her doctoral dissertation, academic neutrality on poverty is not so neutral.

> The problem with the neutrality—the acultural and ahistorical nature of Piaget's theory—is that the social and the historical have a real impact on children's development. It is important to note that when Black and poor girl children are taught, for example, that two plus two equals four, they are also learning through how they are related to, by those around them, both their location within and their relationship to that activity. (Fulani, 1984, p. 10)

NEW DIRECTIONS FOR HIGHER EDUCATION, no. 171, Fall 2015 © 2015 Wiley Periodicals, Inc.
Published online in Wiley Online Library (wileyonlinelibrary.com) • DOI: 10.1002/he.20143

This sentiment is echoed by Confrey (1995), who studied mathematics education from a sociocultural-historical viewpoint:

> Allowing mathematics to continue to require students to disengage from their personal sources of experience and to learn a system of rituals that makes little sense to them but which will admit them to the ranks of the elite is one of the most effective ways of maintaining this oppression. (Confrey, 1995, p. 41)

We have discovered that development of a diverse professoriate requires contexts as described by Fulani (2013). Here we examine the relationship between mentoring and development in the context of the Applied Mathematical Sciences Summer Institute (AMSSI) mentoring model. This Research Experiences for Undergraduates (REU) program, supported by the National Security Agency (NSA) and the National Science Foundation (NSF), was unique in that it focused on nontraditional participants, with explicit attention to participants' emotional and social growth, and improved the capacity of the existing professoriate to increase diversity in their own programs and institutions.

We are practitioners experienced in mentoring diverse student populations, creating environments for their overall growth, learning, and development with an emphasis on having them pursue careers in science, technology, engineering, and mathematics (STEM). We view our work from a Vygotskian perspective that sees learning and development as a dialectical activity in which learning appears first socially and then individually (Holzman, 2010; Newman & Holzman, 1993; Vygotsky, 1978).

> Every function in the child's cultural development appears twice: first on the social level and later, on the individual level; first between people (interpsychological), and then inside the child (intrapsychological). This applies equally to all voluntary attention, to logical memory, and to the formation of concepts. All the higher mental functions originate as actual relations between people. (Vygotsky, 1978, p. 57)

Mentoring is creating a "zone of proximal development," defined as:

> The distance between the actual developmental level as determined by independent problem solving, and the level of potential development as determined through problem solving under guidance or in collaboration with more capable peers. (Vygotsky, 1978, p. 86)

AMSSI's structure supported collaborative relationships to be built among students and faculty as capable peers on multiple dimensions, such as knowledge of the field, emotional skills, critical thinking, and ability

NEW DIRECTIONS FOR HIGHER EDUCATION • DOI: 10.1002/he

to collaborate and work independently. Participants co-created the zone of proximal development through the nature of the dialogue, the focus on building a learning environment together, and each person contributing to the program culture. This collaborative community is most closely related to the definition of mentoring provided by Hendricks (1996):

> In the mentoring role, you 'come alongside' the people on your team ... a mentor is to develop new abilities in the people you work with ... it's a process of development ... it must be built on three components: mutual trust and commitment, patient leadership, and emotional maturity. (Hendricks, 1996, pp. 127–128)

AMSSI's mentoring model is focused on creating the learning community in which all individuals provide leadership to their own learning and the learning of others. This developmental process radically includes their individual cultural and socioeconomic experiences in building the co-created environment.

The importance of focusing on individuals from underrepresented minority (URM) groups is supported by data. In 2000, URMs made up 24.8% of the U.S. population (and are estimated to be 31.9% in 2025). Women made up over half the population. Yet URMs (14%) and women (46%) are underrepresented among holders of bachelor's degrees in mathematics. Among REU participants, over 50% of REU programs have less than 40% URMs, with an average of 38% women and 9% URMs (see Table 7.1). With many graduate schools expecting students to have some undergraduate research experience, REUs can be a key mechanism for getting students into graduate programs.

Table 7.1. Percentage of Women and URMs in Mathematics REU Programs and Receiving PhDs

	Total Number of Participants	% Women	% URMs
Through 1999			
All REU programs	1,931	36%	12%
REU programs with less than 40% URM participants	1,702	34%	3%
2000 through 2006			
All REU programs	881	43%	26%
REU programs with less than 40% URM participants	560	38%	9%
Math bachelor's degrees awarded (2000)	11,800	46%	14%
Math PhDs awarded (U.S. citizen and permanent resident, 1997–2004)	3,663	31.3%	5.7%

Sources: REU data in Gallian (2007). PhD data in Petersen, Kraus, and Windham (2005); Notices of American Mathematical Society (1999–2005).

Philosophy and Perspective on Learning and Development in Context

The NSF is keenly aware of problems created by underrepresentation. To better prepare the next generation, the NSF has invested in REUs. We uniquely and strongly address NSF's objective of integrating "research and education to attract a diversified pool of talented students into careers in science." AMSSI's goal is to develop PhD mathematicians who are URMs, female, or individuals from nonresearch or nonselective schools who will impact the culture and diversity of the United States while also strengthening the communities from which they come. We acknowledge that the collective experiences of the faculty (Fox, Sonnert, & Nikiforova, 2009) shaped the structure and goals of AMSSI. Although our philosophical and political thinking has been produced by our particular histories, our particular histories are not required to adopt these approaches. In this work, we highlight the strategic intentions for each element of AMSSI in hopes of making transparent our thinking and posture.

We firmly believe that diversity in REUs should focus on students who might not otherwise have the opportunity. Simply placing URM students in an REU that provides research opportunities might be an effective way of retaining these students in STEM fields. Programs must take into account who people are socially and culturally and that experiences differ. Thus the AMSSI model builds students' subjective relationship to research and learning while it also cultivates students' creativity and imagination, builds their self-esteem, fosters interaction with people of different backgrounds, and provides a support network of caring mentors and role models (Brown, Collins, & Duguid, 1989).

We create an environment that supports participants' learning as well as their development. By development, we mean the ability of people to see and make choices on behalf of their own growth. It has been our experience that to promote their growth and empowerment it is important to stretch students by taking them out of their familiar elements, but also to provide components of familiarity. A unique feature of AMSSI that exemplifies our commitment to the complete development of students is the weekly meetings for sharing personal experiences, detailed in a later section. The stretching and feedback are an integral part of faculty, mentors, and peers working alongside one another to create their learning. As Holzman (2010) indicates, we relate to what they are *becoming*. They are both who they are, from schools or neighborhoods that have limited access to academic research or mathematics, and who they are becoming, students capable of mathematics research and discourse. We give explicit recognition to collaboration, community, and emotional growth as central to students becoming (performing as) mathematicians (Eisenhart & Finkel, 1998; Lave & Wenger, 1991; Tavernise, 2012; Wenger, 1998).

NEW DIRECTIONS FOR HIGHER EDUCATION • DOI: 10.1002/he

The REU Academic Environment

AMSSI was held at California State Polytechnic University, Pomona, and at Loyola Marymount University. The schools' locations within the greater Los Angeles area provided two different academic climates and experiences. Here we define the structural elements and subjective features of AMSSI that are critical to developing a diverse professoriate.

Recruitment of Students.   To achieve diversity in our program, it is essential to recruit from a very wide pool of talented students. We targeted schools with a large percentage of women and/or URMs, including all-women colleges, historically Black colleges and universities (HBCUs), Hispanic-serving institutions (HSIs), Native American tribal colleges, public universities near large cities, and community colleges. We used flyers, e-mails, local newspapers, and especially personal contacts to inform faculty and students about this opportunity. We chose a program start date (usually in early June) to permit students from quarter-based calendar schools to apply to and attend AMSSI.

The AMSSI faculty actively recruited at conferences with attendees diverse in their socioeconomic and ethnic backgrounds and in their fields of study, including the SACNAS Conference, the Joint Math Meetings, and the Infinite Possibilities Conference. Talking one on one with prospective students built relationships important to the program's sustainability. This first step in building an experience that affects their lives builds the professoriate pipeline (Merriam, 1983) where these students become future colleagues who participate in the network of student research and development.

Student Selection.   We focused on students who would benefit most from participating. We looked for evidence that an applicant might be a first-generation college student, indicators of low economic status, and lack of research opportunities at their own institutions, and we placed emphasis on letters of recommendation and personal statements. Applications were reviewed by all AMSSI faculty members, each of whom sought different characteristics of diversity. This maximized the potential for choosing a diverse student group.

Partnerships and Exposure to Industrial and Nontraditional Mathematics.   We facilitated the building of a functioning support network for students by having them interact in nontrivial ways with as many partnering faculty members and potential employers as possible. We arranged partnerships with select NSF-sponsored programs in the mathematical sciences (such as the Integrative Graduate Education and Research Traineeship [IGERT] program) to strengthen the pipeline from undergraduate to graduate school. We hosted colloquia by these individuals who are known to be great mentors and role models and had them speak on why they pursued a PhD in STEM. Students asked them to talk frankly about graduate school and PhD programs at their respective institutions. In each interaction, the students got to know the graduate programs from insiders, could imagine themselves in the graduate program, and could see it as part of their academic community.

Additional information was provided in various forms. A comprehensive, thorough 4-hour interactive session was led by an expert on the graduate school application process. We presented numerous other employment opportunities that excited and encouraged our students to pursue higher degrees. Representatives of these industries presented on applications of mathematics in their corporations. We also exposed students to the UCLA Department of Human Genetics with presentations on the interplay of mathematics and genetics.

Math Boot Camp.   The first week of AMSSI was particularly intense. "Math boot camp" days lasted from 8 a.m. to 12 midnight. We had 4 hours of interactive lecture and problem sessions, followed by a 4-hour interactive computer lab. Students worked in pairs, changing partners for each lab. During the evenings, the students had a fairly difficult homework assignment. Only by working with each other, with help from faculty and graduate research associates, did the students finish the assignment in a reasonable amount of time. Through this schedule and need to work together, students and faculty gained an appreciation of one another's strengths and weaknesses, as well as practice getting help from and giving help to each other. This prepared them for the next 6 weeks.

Open Weekly Research Meetings.   Since most AMSSI students were conducting research for the first time and came from nonresearch institutions, we gave them frequent feedback. The student research groups met and worked with their advisors on a daily basis. They gave group presentations of their work at weekly research meetings to the AMSSI faculty, visitors (including colloquium speakers), and campus faculty. Presenting helped the students reinforce what they had learned, better understand their research problems, think on their feet, practice their oral presentation skills, and generate value (for students and community) that goes beyond a grade. Our focus on group performance allowed for knowledge to appear socially with all (experts, novices, visitors, etc.), not just as it relates to the individual student but as it relates to the overall scientific community.

Fostering a Collaborative Learning Community

Building a diverse collaborative learning community is an intentional practice. Diversity requires creating ways of using and building with existing differences rather than ignoring them. Research suggests that many of our students would typically have to disengage from their personal experiences in their efforts to pursue their goals of attaining a higher degree (Confrey, 1995, p. 41). This in turn will have detrimental effects on their learning capacity. Recognizing this experience, we chose from the beginning to

NEW DIRECTIONS FOR HIGHER EDUCATION • DOI: 10.1002/he

ensure that the AMSSI experience would be one in which our students' emotional growth parallels their academic growth. We agree with the following statement:

> The introduction of emotional intelligence into discussions of mathematics education allows one to assert that both facilitating and debilitating emotions play a significant role in learning, and that emotional qualities of classroom interactions will exert a significant influence on what is learned. (Confrey, 1995, p. 39)

A key step in incorporating emotional growth into the AMSSI experience was weekly sharing meetings, which were attended by student participants and the AMSSI faculty. In these meetings, each member shared some of his or her personal side, including significant life experiences, dreams, fears, extreme obstacles that had been overcome, upbringing, family background, role models, hobbies, and so on. Only AMSSI students and faculty attended the meetings so as to maintain a culture of confidentiality, trust, and respect that we carefully built throughout the program. These meetings established human connections between the faculty and students that carried over into their work. This type of personal interaction highlights the importance of keeping life in perspective and in balance. By the end of the program, everyone had had the opportunity to ask questions, have questions asked of them, and share a personal side of them that otherwise would not have been possible to share outside of this setting. The emotional intensity of the weekly sharing meetings complemented the intensity we required for the academic aspects of AMSSI.

Program events were held about once a week, often an off-campus excursion that combined an academic and a nonacademic activity. For example, we had research presentations by mathematicians at DreamWorks Studios and then went to Universal Studios for the remainder of the day. To give equal weight to the varied life experiences of our students and faculty, these excursions included trips to poorer neighborhoods. From research to cultural excursions, we were consistently cognizant of the goal to give participants the ability to use their own and one another's experiences to create a context for their growth.

From the first day of the program, we stressed that AMSSI is a team effort and a learning community in which everyone benefits. In the second week, the faculty placed students into groups of four and begin focused background lectures for the student research projects. Then the research groups made the transition from classroom theory to independent research. A complete written draft of each group's work was due at the end of the sixth week. The students received written feedback, made corrections, and gave oral presentations to the academic communities on both campuses.

A key to AMSSI's success was the dedication of its faculty, who had seen, either as a student or as a faculty member, the impact that undergraduate research can have on developing students. Faculty ownership of the program was fostered from the beginning and was essential for success in this time-intensive environment. Educating and mentoring the whole person includes mentors and mentees sharing life experiences, connecting emotions and familiarity to new knowledge, fostering individual growth, building trust, creating a strong community, and making work a team effort in which everyone contributes and benefits.

By experiencing students in contexts beyond academics, our own assumptions about what students are capable of achieving changed because we got to know them as whole and capable beings. This subjective experience changes how we work with students. Faculty member Ed Mosteig learned this from his AMSSI experience: "Many of the academic challenges encountered by my students stem from issues that they wrestle with in their personal lives, and often those issues need to be addressed first. More so than ever, I try to get to know 'the whole person' before mentoring and advising" (personal communication, November 7, 2013).

Visiting faculty and program directors are also changed in their understanding of what is needed for students from less advantaged backgrounds to grow and become academically accomplished. Visiting faculty participant David Manderscheid has developed an appreciation for the whole student: "Community matters to the students, and it matters to how they do mathematics." Where we come from affects our perspective on problems and how we reason from one step to another, he says, so increasing diversity also increases awareness that there is more than one way to look at and understand mathematical problems (personal communication, November 2, 2013).

Exemplary Results

AMSSI ran from 2005 through 2007, with many successes (see http://www.public.asu.edu/~etcamach/AMSSI/). Four of these projects were published in refereed journals (Abiva et al., 2007; Anderson, Byrne, Fields, Segovia, & Swift, 2008; Bewernick, Dewar, Gray, Rodriguez, & Swift, 2007; Gallegos et al., 2008). The students gave poster presentations at SACNAS conferences and the Joint Math Meetings. At the latter conference, five of 12 groups won poster awards.

Our success is best captured by the percentage of students who participated in AMSSI who (a) have gone on to graduate school, (b) have completed a graduate degree (MS, PhD), (c) work in an applied mathematics or other STEM field, or (d) have entered the professoriate. AMSSI had 16 to 18 students per year, and 39 of the 52 participants have gone on to graduate school. Some 35% are expected to receive PhDs by the time of this publication; over 70% will have an MS or higher degree. More than 10% of all

NEW DIRECTIONS FOR HIGHER EDUCATION • DOI: 10.1002/he

AMSSI participants are employed as instructors, lecturers, or professors at schools of higher education.

Conclusion

The AMSSI program creates an environment in which students develop in their ability to see the professoriate, to see themselves in it, and to be able to make choices that foster their career development. An essential part of creating that development is fostering functional relationships among all faculty and students. We created a context in which students were able to ask professionals in the field not only how to achieve technical success but how they made the life choices that went with building their careers. The words *interact*, *get to know*, and *exposed to* are too small for the quality of conversations and relationships built among visitors, the program, and the students. We see the success of these relationships in AMSSI students accepted and graduating from graduate programs. We cannot overstress the importance of strategically creating environments that foster relationships among all participants, and that accept where students come from and together create where they are going.

Faculty, visitors, and students create academic culture together that is inclusive of everyone's history and societal background. Key skills of faculty to build inclusive, collaborative environments that make use of the diverse backgrounds of themselves and their students include a willingness to learn from and alongside students and to provide expectations consistent with who the students are (discovered in the context of the program) and who they are becoming (capable mathematician scientists). The directors learned this approach through their early professional experiences and created their own variation with explicit attention to socioemotional development. To replicate such a program, there's a need to invest in the professional development and retention of faculty who can create and build such developmental programs. Successful programs require institutional commitment to both program and faculty.

References

Abiva, J., Camacho, E., Joseph, E., Mikaelian, A., Rogers, C., Shelton, J., & Wirkus, S. (2007). Alcohol's effect on neuron firing. *Mathematical Scientist*, 32(1), 32–40.

Anderson, J., Byrne, A., Fields, R., Segovia, L., & Swift, R. (2008). A simple stochastic epidemic process with total quarantine of infectives. *Applied Mathematical Sciences*, 2(16), 753–761.

Bewernick, R., Dewar, J., Gray, E., Rodriguez, N., & Swift, R. (2007). On the representation of birth-death processes with polynomial transition rates. *Journal of Statistical Theory and Practice*, 1(2), 227–231.

Brown, J., Collins, A., & Duguid, P. (1989). Situated cognition and the culture of learning. *Educational Researcher*, 18, 32–42.

Confrey, J. (1995). A theory of intellectual development, Part III. *For the Learning of Mathematics, 15*(2), 36–45.

Eisenhart, M., & Finkel, E. (1998). *Women's science: Learning and succeeding from the margins.* Chicago, IL: University of Chicago Press.

Fox, M. F., Sonnert, G., & Nikiforova, I. (2009). Successful programs for undergraduate women in science and engineering: Adapting vs. adopting the institutional environment. *Research in Higher Education, 50,* 303–353.

Fulani, L. B. (1984). *Children's understanding of number symbols in formal and informal contexts* (Unpublished doctoral dissertation). Graduate Center of the City University of New York, New York, NY.

Fulani, L. B. (2013, April). *The development line: Helping the poor to grow: A special report on solving the poverty crisis in America.* Paper presented at American Education Research Association, San Francisco, CA.

Gallegos, A., Plummer, T., Uminsky, D., Vega, C., Wickman, C., & Zawoiski, M. (2008). A mathematical model of a crocodilian population using delay-differential equations. *Journal Mathematical Biology, 57,* 737–754.

Gallian, J. A. (2007). Survey of undergraduate research programs. In J. A. Gallian (Ed.), *Proceedings of the Conference on Summer Undergraduate Mathematics Research Programs* (pp. 399–451). Providence, RI: American Mathematical Society.

Hendricks, W. (Ed.). (1996). *Coaching, mentoring and managing: Breakthrough strategies to solve performance problems and build winning teams.* Franklin Lakes, NJ: Career Press.

Holzman, L. (2010). Without creating ZPDs there is no creativity. In C. Connery, V. John-Steiner, & A. Marjanovic-Shane (Eds.), *Vygotsky and creativity: A cultural-historical approach to play, meaning making, and the arts* (pp. 27–40). New York, NY: Peter Lang Publishing.

Lave, J., & Wenger, E. (1991). *Situated learning: Legitimate peripheral participation.* Cambridge, UK: Cambridge University Press.

Merriam, S. (1983). Mentors and proteges: A critical review of the literature. *Adult Education Quarterly, 33*(3), 161–173.

Newman, F., & Holzman, L. (1993). *Lev Vygotsky: Revolutionary scientist.* London, UK: Routledge.

Notices of the American Mathematical Society. (1999–2005, February).

Petersen, M. R., Kraus, B. E., & Windham T. L. (2005, March). Striving toward equity: Underrepresented minorities and mathematics. *SIAM News, 38*(2), 1–3. Retrieved from http://www.siam.org/pdf/news/29.pdf

Tavernise, S. (2012, February 9). Education gap grows between rich and poor, study says. *New York Times.* Retrieved from http://www.nytimes.com/2012/02/10/education/education-gap-grows-between-rich-and-poor-studies-show.html

U.S. Census Bureau. (2011). People in poverty by selected characteristics. Washington, DC: Author. Retrieved from http://www.census.gov/hhes/www/poverty/data/incpov hlth/2011/table3.pdf

Vygotsky, L. (1978). *Mind in society: The development of higher psychological processes.* Cambridge, MA: Harvard University Press.

Wenger, E. (1998). *Communities of practice: Learning, meaning and identity.* Cambridge, UK: Cambridge University Press.

ERIKA T. CAMACHO, cofounder of AMSSI, is currently an MLK Visiting Professor in the Department of Mathematics at the Massachusetts Institute of Technology and an associate professor at Arizona State University.

RAQUELL M. HOLMES is the director and founder of improvscience as well as research assistant professor in the Center for Computational Science at Boston University.

STEPHEN A. WIRKUS, cofounder of AMSSI, is currently an MLK Visiting Professor in the Department of Mathematics at the Massachusetts Institute of Technology and an associate professor in the School of Mathematical and Natural Sciences at Arizona State University.

NEW DIRECTIONS FOR HIGHER EDUCATION • DOI: 10.1002/he

This chapter highlights the development of Project MALES (Mentoring to Achieve Latino Educational Success). At the center of Project MALES is a mentoring program that aims to cultivate an engaged support network for males of color at the University of Texas at Austin and across surrounding communities. Specifically, there is a discussion of the theories and framework that guided the creation of this mentoring program and its ongoing development.

Developing a Latino Mentoring Program: Project MALES (Mentoring to Achieve Latino Educational Success)

Victor B. Sáenz, Luis Ponjuan, Jorge Segovia Jr., José Del Real Viramontes

The long-term educational success for Latino male students and other males of color has become a recent focus of state and federal policy initiatives. While the number of Latinos attending college and attaining degrees has increased steadily in recent years, the proportional representation of Latino males enrolled in higher education continues to lag behind their female peers (Sáenz & Ponjuan, 2009). In 2012, Latino males had the lowest high school graduation rates across all male ethnic groups, and more than 60% of all associate's or bachelor's degrees earned by Hispanics were earned by female students (U.S. Census Bureau, 2013). These trends suggest that, compared to their peers, Latino males continue to face challenges in achieving critical higher education milestones.

In 2014 President Obama announced a new initiative called "My Brother's Keeper," which mobilized resources and support from public, private, and foundation organizations to address the persistent educational attainment gap for males of color. Until recently this educational issue had largely gone unnoticed or underexamined by policy makers and education leaders, with little to no focus on Latino males in spite of the shifting demographic trends across the country (Sáenz & Ponjuan, 2011). The lack of critical awareness about the challenges of changing student demographics, especially for Latino males, underscores the urgency of this issue. Ultimately, a lack of proactive efforts to address the unique needs of Latino

NEW DIRECTIONS FOR HIGHER EDUCATION, no. 171, Fall 2015 © 2015 Wiley Periodicals, Inc.
Published online in Wiley Online Library (wileyonlinelibrary.com) • DOI: 10.1002/he.20144

males in the educational system has untold implications for the future economic and social prosperity of the country and the well-being of the nation's fastest growing population segment, the Latina/o community.

With these challenges in mind (and guided by our research), we conceived a mentoring program to help Latino males in local middle schools and high schools more effectively navigate their educational journeys. This provided the impetus for a research and mentoring program that focuses explicitly on Latino males in the education pipeline—it is called Project MALES.

Project MALES

Project MALES (Mentoring to Achieve Latino Educational Success) officially launched in the fall of 2010 as a new research and mentoring initiative within the Division of Diversity and Community Engagement (DDCE) at the University of Texas at Austin (UT-Austin). Project MALES encompasses three interrelated initiatives: an ongoing research project focused on exploring the experiences of Latino males across the education pipeline, a mentoring program that aims to cultivate an engaged support network for males of color, and a new statewide P–16 Consortium focused on leveraging shared strategies to ensure the success of male of color across Texas (see Figure 8.1).

Project MALES embodies praxis by fusing these initiatives through mentoring, research, collective impact, and dissemination to research and

Figure 8.1. Project MALES Programmatic Structure

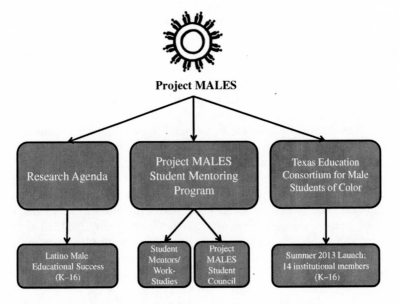

practitioner communities. For example, our mentoring model emerged directly from our research findings and our review of the mentoring literature; it highlights near-peer and intergenerational mentoring as strategies to leverage social capital among Latino males across multiple generations and in both secondary and postsecondary contexts. Project MALES is focused on the overarching goal of enhancing male student success throughout the educational spectrum. To this end, our chapter focuses specifically on the research and mentoring philosophy behind our Project MALES Student Mentoring Program.

The model is distinct for several reasons: it explicitly focuses on Latino males; it is largely influenced by best practices on mentoring males of color; it is informed by our ongoing multiyear research efforts on Latino males; and it highlights a unique collaboration between a public research university and several local educational and community partners. Our ultimate aim is to inspire others to take action and respond to the growing national imperative for Latino males in education.

Conceptual Theories and Models of Mentoring

The impetus for our Project MALES Student Mentoring Program is discussed through the examination of existing mentoring models and theories, especially those that focus on males of color. These models included *cross-age mentoring, intergenerational mentoring, natural mentoring, developmental mentoring, instrumental mentoring, community-based mentoring* (CBM), and *school-based mentoring* (SBM). Many of these were not specific to male students, but it was beneficial to understand the predominant theories and models of mentoring that would shape the development of our Project MALES Student Mentoring Program. In this section, we provide some of the characteristics and benefits for each mentoring model, and we also discuss the curriculum, practices, and programs specific to men that were important for us to consider as we designed our model. Whether it was *cross-age mentoring, intergenerational mentoring,* or *community-/school-based mentoring*, studying such models guided our development of a unique mentoring effort focused on improving educational outcomes for Latino males.

Cross-Age Mentoring.   *Cross-age mentoring* is described as a mentor of middle school or high school age (a youth at least 2 years older than the child being mentored) and a mentee meeting regularly, usually weekly, for a sustained, consistent period of time (minimally 10 times; ideally 20 or more times) to engage in conversations, play, or curricula/structured activities (ones that do not directly or solely teach information or skills in which the mentee has been found lacking) that help forge a close relationship in which the mentee experiences empathy, praise, and attention from the mentor (Karcher, 2014).

Intergenerational Mentoring.   *Intergenerational mentoring* is a mentoring relationship in which youths are mentored by adults 55 years of age or older. This type of mentoring relationship is beneficial to both, seeing that for the older adult, this creates an opportunity to pass along skills and knowledge to the young person and at the same time validate his or her own life experiences (Karcher, Kuperminc, Portwood, Sipe, & Taylor, 2006). Characteristics of successful intergenerational mentoring relationships include having frequent contact, and preferably lasting a year or more (Grossman & Johnson, 1999).

Natural Mentoring.   *Natural mentoring* is characterized as mentoring between youths and nonparental adults, including extended family members, teachers, or neighbors, from whom a young person receives support and guidance as a result of a relationship developed without the support of a program designed to connect youths and adults to form a mentoring relationship. One of the benefits of this type of mentoring model that the authors highlight is the organic nature of the relationship that the youth and adult mentor develop. This allows for the possibility of a longer-lasting relationship. In the long run, youths who engage in this type of mentoring relationship can develop the confidence and capabilities to engage with other nonparental adults, and can benefit from those relationships (Zimmerman, Bingenheimer, & Behrendt, 2005).

Developmental Mentoring.   In *developmental mentoring*, the focus is on the development of the mentee–mentor relationship, with the objective of promoting the social, emotional, and academic development of the youth. This form of mentoring is characterized by the mentor getting involved in recreational activities with the mentee, like playing games. In a developmental mentoring relationship, the mentor's goal is to develop the conditions in the relationship that would allow the youth's social, cognitive, and emotional development (Karcher et al., 2006).

Instrumental Mentoring.   *Instrumental mentoring* is characterized by a more structured mentee–mentor relationship where specific skills are to be gained, or specific achievements to be fulfilled during the term of the relationship. This relationship provides more guidance. Some of the tasks or goals of this type of relationship can be encouraging the mentee to engage in a predetermined task, including goal setting to achieve certain academic skills, or decreasing risk-taking behavior. In certain contexts, this type of relationship can be more beneficial in the youth's development (Karcher et al., 2006).

Community- and School-Based Mentoring Programs.   Hall (2006) describes two types of mentoring programs: *community-based mentoring* (CBM) and *school-based mentoring* (SBM) programs. Hall describes the CBM approach as traditionally bringing a mentor and mentee together for one-on-one mentoring. Mentor/mentee matching is usually based on race, cultural background, shared economic status, life experiences, spoken language, and gender. Hall reveals that children and adolescents who participate in CBM programs are less likely to engage in using illegal drugs, using alcohol, skipping school, and participating in violence; the CBM programs help build their self-esteem and a sense of belonging with school, peers, and family.

Similarly, the SBM programs provide youths with safe and supervised surroundings where they may experience a sense of belonging through peer support and interaction. Through the SBM model, students learn both how to operate in their interpersonal world but also how to collaborate with others to develop strategies for dealing with their academic and personal issues. Since SBM programs are group-based models, this gives adults the opportunity to connect with more students at one specific time. SBM programs offer students additional adult support in the school environment. Students who participate in an SBM program may experience an enhanced feeling of belonging, higher academic achievement, a broadening of classroom knowledge, increased self-identification, and decreased levels of delinquency or violence (Hall, 2006, p. 13).

Mentoring Models Specific to Male Students of Color.   In regard to mentoring males of color, Reddick, Heilig, Marks, and Crosby (2012) suggest the use of two key theoretical concepts, *social exchange theory* and *mentoring networks*, to describe how these tools have translated into the success of Black males. They argue that each theoretical concept offers a benefit to mentoring Black males. For example, they suggest that in using social exchange theory both mentors and mentees must find mutual benefit and satisfaction in the relationship. They also suggest that mentoring networks allow the mentee to develop and utilize a network of supportive mentors versus having only one. This network of mentors provides the mentee with access to multiple sources of social capital. This research highlights the importance of understanding the delicate and dynamic nature of mentoring. We acknowledge and infuse these mentoring concepts in the ongoing development of our Project MALES Student Mentoring Program.

Mentoring Research Focused on Latino Students

We also reviewed research literature on adult mentors and role models and their relationships with Latino youths. Sánchez, Esparza, and Colón (2008) examined the role of *natural mentoring relationships* (NMRs) in the academic performance of Latino adolescents. Their study revealed that most of youths' NMRs were with immediate and extended family members. For these students, having a mentor translated into positive academic outcomes, including greater expectancy of success, higher educational expectations, fewer absences, and a greater sense of school belonging. In addition, having support from multiple mentors was also an important contribution to their academic success. In their qualitative interviews with 10 Mexican American adolescents, Sánchez, Reyes, and Singh (2006) identified four benefits as a result of strong mentoring relationships: *intrapersonal development*, *interpersonal development*, *school-related benefits*, and *behavioral benefits*.

NEW DIRECTIONS FOR HIGHER EDUCATION • DOI: 10.1002/he

We also were informed by mentoring research that described how youths selected and identified potential mentors and/or role models. In their study, which evaluated the social networks and help-seeking practices of Mexican-origin youths in San Diego, California, Stanton-Salazar and Spina (2003) revealed that, for these youths, certain developed criteria (e.g., *social class*, *racial status*, *ethnic status*, and *gender*) were important determinant characteristics when adolescents selected their role models. Another important characteristic they used to select mentors was validating messages from caring adults who had overcome similar obstacles.

An important period in determining the success of Latina/o students is when they transition from high school into college. Sánchez, Esparza, Berardi, and Pryce (2011) highlight the importance of having a supportive network or a natural mentor during the transition of youths from high school into college. Students who had mentors at both points (e.g., during and after high school) had a resource-high social network, which helped them with their transitions. In contrast, students who did not have a mentor at both points or had no mentors at all were described by the authors as having resource-limited social networks (usually immediate family only), which meant having limited and often vague support from fewer individuals in the transitions beyond high school.

Once in college, the importance of mentoring Latina/o college students continues to be critical in their degree completion (Bordes & Arrendondo, 2005). In their implementation and evaluation of a pilot mentoring program that focused on matching graduate students with incoming Latino college freshmen who were considered at risk for poor academic outcomes, Campos et al. (2009) reveal four areas of the short-term effects of the program: having an *increase of social support*, feeling that they had *increased general knowledge and awareness of the resources* that were available to them, an *increased awareness of their academic skills* (which are important for academic success and long-term educational/educational career options), and their *overall positive adjustment to college* (p. 171). A similar study (Phinney, Campos, Cidhinnia, Padilla Kallemeyn, & Kim, 2011) found that students who were mentored by upper-level students (i.e., third and fourth year) compared to those students who were not mentored did not display a decline in their academic motivation, were less depressed, and had lower levels of stress.

Finally, although not directly related to Latino students, Yosso (2005) offers a fundamental contribution to the development of the Project MALES Student Mentoring Program. She argues that communities of color have the potential to offer an "array of cultural knowledge, skills, abilities and contacts" that can greatly benefit individuals from socially marginalized groups (p. 69). We embrace this conceptualization of "cultural capital" and suggest that student mentors of color can offer a wealth of support (e.g., tangible and intangible) to other students of color—especially Latino males—as they navigate their educational pathways.

Project MALES Student Mentoring Program

The Project MALES Student Mentoring Program connects Latino male undergraduate students from UT-Austin (and allies) with males of color in local area middle schools and high schools. The program operates with the following goals/objectives: (1) to develop and sustain a research-informed, culturally relevant mentoring program that is linked to the academic core of UT-Austin; (2) to increase year-to-year retention as well as graduation rates of Latino undergraduate students enrolled at UT-Austin who participate as mentors; (3) to engage with community partners to raise awareness about the unique challenges facing Latino males and males of color across the educational pipeline; and (4) to provide culturally relevant guidance to encourage lifelong learning for high school and undergraduate Latino males and other males of color.

In an effort to anchor our mentoring curriculum and training to the academic core, Project MALES requires all of its undergraduate student mentors to enroll in a service-learning course called Instructing Males through Peer Advising College Tracks (IMPACT). This yearlong course focuses on mentoring young men of color, and the course objectives are to enhance college student engagement and academic achievement by offering active and experiential learning opportunities through near peer advising and service learning for our undergraduate student mentors. This course helps our undergraduate student mentors build a robust knowledge base on mentoring research and gain important insights about the challenges facing males of color in education. We also use the course to deploy our mentoring curriculum and to engage in weekly reflections on mentoring activities. IMPACT emphasizes active learning in different environments, allows students to see and experience the relationship between theory and practice, and provides students with opportunities to use newly acquired knowledge and skills in real-life mentoring situations.

Once out in the field, our Project MALES undergraduate student mentors work with their mentees in an effort to improve the educational attainment and college-going competencies of young men of color while also providing a safe space for these students to discuss questions related to going to college. Mentors visit with local middle school and high school students most weeks throughout the academic year to mentor and discuss a variety of topics ranging from college preparation to financial literacy to the "soft" skills necessary to succeed in college and beyond.

The mentoring program currently partners directly with the Austin Independent School District and serves four high schools and one middle school within the district, delivering over 1,600 hours of mentoring per year to over 50 males of color. Coupled with our many community engagement activities throughout the academic year (e.g., hosting campus tours, Feria Para Aprender, Explore UT), our undergraduate student mentors easily reach hundreds more young males of color across the state. We are also fortunate to engage in joint programming with other male-focused initiatives in the region, such as the UT-Austin African American Male Research Initiative (AAMRI), the XY-Zone boys program (Communities in Schools in Central Texas), and LaunchPad, all of which also serve adolescent males with leadership and mentoring opportunities.

An additional mentoring component of our model that builds on the near-peer philosophy is the Project MALES Graduate Student Mentoring Program. This component matches undergraduate mentors with current UT-Austin graduate students or professionals to informally explore the unique differences between the undergraduate and graduate study experiences. Since mentoring is done in an informal fashion, graduate mentors visit with undergraduates, based on availability, to discuss topics ranging from the graduate school application process and requirements to how to support oneself financially as a graduate student to the soft skills necessary to succeed in graduate school and beyond.

Mentoring Structure.   The Project MALES Student Mentoring Program fosters discussion and relationship building among male students of color across various age cohorts—middle school and high school students, UT-Austin undergraduate mentors, and UT-Austin graduate mentors (see Figure 8.2). The basic structure entails *near-peer group mentoring* to allow for longer-term bonds to develop between our undergraduate mentors and male middle school and high school students of color participating in the

Figure 8.2. Project MALES Undergraduate and Graduate Student Mentoring Programs—Structure

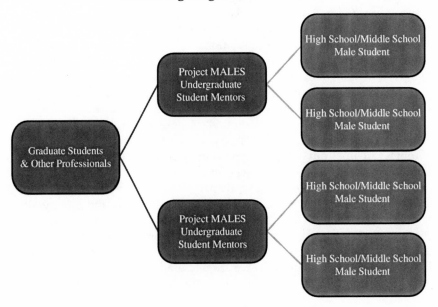

mentoring program. Similarly, the Project MALES Graduate Student Mentoring Program has a basic structure that utilizes informal *one-on-one* or *one-on-two group mentoring* to allow undergraduate mentors an opportunity to connect with graduate students to explore differences between the undergraduate and graduate study experiences.

As mentioned in the discussion of the different mentoring models, Project MALES employs an *intergenerational* and *near-peer* approach to bring about increased achievement and retention of male students of color in both secondary and postsecondary settings. This model brings together three key groups: (1) males of color who are middle school and high school students, (2) Latino male undergraduate students and other student allies, and (3) graduate students and professionals. In this model, graduate students serve as mentors to undergraduate mentors, who in turn mentor male students of color in middle school or high school. This model is structured around a variety of experiences that focus on leadership development, community engagement, and service.

A brief overview of the types of mentoring activities of our Project MALES Student Mentoring Program reveals a depth and breadth of influence across different educational levels. There are many opportunities for students to engage actively in activities that benefit and shape their educational experiences. We propose that the Project MALES Student Mentoring Program offers a unique structure that allows students to engage in authentic and positive personal and professional relationships across generations.

Conclusion

To our knowledge, there are few research or programmatic efforts across the country that address the urgent crisis facing Latino males in education, and the lack of action or critical awareness comes at a time when the Latino community is driving significant demographic shifts across the country. The Project MALES Student Mentoring Program offers a model that can help address the unique challenges of Latino males in education. The model is very much in its infancy, but it is already receiving local and national acclaim for several reasons: it explicitly focuses on Latino males; it is largely influenced by best practices on mentoring adolescent youth as well as an ongoing multiyear research effort on Latino males; and it highlights a unique collaboration between a research-extensive institution and several local educational and community partners.

With a sense of urgency in the national discourse about improving educational outcomes for male students of color, we recognize that lasting change and impact must occur first at the local level. As such, we developed this mentoring model with a strong focus on research, leadership development, and service to our local community. Our goal is for the Project MALES Student Mentoring Program to serve as a model to others in their efforts to enhance male student success across all levels of the educational spectrum.

References

Bordes, V., & Arredondo, P. (2005). Mentoring and 1st-year Latina/o college students. *Journal of Hispanic Higher Education, 4*(2), 114–133.

Campos, C. M. T., Phinney, J. S., Perez-Brena, N., Kim, C., Ornelas, B., Nemanim, L., & Ramirez, C. (2009). A mentor-based targeted intervention for high-risk Latino college freshmen: A pilot study. *Journal of Hispanic Higher Education, 8*(2), 158–178.

Grossman, J. B., & Johnson, A. W. (1999). Assessing the effectiveness of mentoring programs. In J. B. Grossman (Ed.), *Contemporary issues in mentoring* (pp. 48–65). Philadelphia, PA: Public/Private Ventures.

Hall, H. R. (2006). *Mentoring young men of color: Meeting the needs of African American and Latino students.* Lanham, MD: Roman & Littlefield Education.

Karcher, M. J. (2014). Cross-age peer mentoring. In D. L. DuBois & M. J. Karcher (Eds.), *Handbook of youth mentoring* (pp. 266–286). Thousand Oaks, CA: SAGE Publications.

Karcher, M. J., Kuperminc, G. P., Portwood, S. G., Sipe, C. L., & Taylor, A. S. (2006). Mentoring programs: A framework to inform program development, research, and evaluation. *Journal of Community Psychology, 34*(6), 709–725.

Phinney, J. S., Campos, T., Cidhinnia, M., Padilla Kallemeyn, D. M., & Kim, C. (2011). Processes and outcomes of a mentoring program for Latino college freshmen. *Journal of Social Issues, 67*(3), 599–621.

Reddick, R. J., Heilig, J. V., Marks, B. T., & Crosby, B. (2012). The current and dire state of African American male crime and education in the central southwest: Are mentoring constellations a promising strategy? *Journal of African American Males in Education, 3*(1), 29–46.

Sáenz, V. B., & Ponjuan, L. (2009). The vanishing Latino male in higher education. *Journal of Hispanic Higher Education, 8*(54), 54–89.

Sáenz, V. B., & Ponjuan, L. (2011). *Men of color: Ensuring the academic success of Latino males in higher education.* Washington, DC: Institute for Higher Education Policy.

Sánchez, B., Esparza, P., Berardi, L., & Pryce, J. (2011). Mentoring and the broader village in the transition from high school. *Youth & Society, 43*(1), 225–252.

Sánchez, B., Esparza, P., & Colón, Y. (2008). Natural mentoring under the microscope: An investigation of mentoring relationships and Latino adolescents' academic performance. *Journal of Community Psychology, 36*(4), 468–482.

Sánchez, B., Reyes, O., & Singh, J. (2006). A qualitative examination of the relationships that serve a mentoring function for Mexican American older adolescents. *Cultural Diversity and Ethnic Minority Psychology, 12*(4), 615–631.

Stanton-Salazar, R. D., & Spina, S. U. (2003). Informal mentors and role models in the lives of urban Mexican-origin adolescents. *Anthropology & Education Quarterly, 34*(3), 231–254.

U.S. Census Bureau. (2013). Table 1: Educational attainment of the population 18 years and over, by age, sex, race, and Hispanic origin: 2013. *Current Population Survey, 2013 Annual Social and Economic Supplement.* Washington, DC: Author.

Yosso, T. J. (2005). Whose culture has capital? A critical race theory discussion of community cultural wealth. *Race, Ethnicity, and Education, 8*(1), 69–91.

Zimmerman, M. A., Bingenheimer, J. B., & Behrendt, D. E. (2005). Natural mentoring relationships. In D. L. DuBois & M. J. Karcher (Eds.), *Handbook of youth mentoring* (pp. 143–157). Thousand Oaks, CA: Sage.

VICTOR B. SÁENZ is the executive director and founder of Project MALES within the Division of Diversity and Community Engagement at the University of Texas at Austin, and an associate professor of educational administration at UT-Austin.

LUIS PONJUAN is cofounder of Project MALES and an associate professor at Texas A&M University.

JORGE SEGOVIA JR. is the curriculum & engagement coordinator for Project MALES and a graduate student at the University of Texas at Austin.

JOSÉ DEL REAL VIRAMONTES is a research associate for Project MALES and a graduate student at the University of Texas at Austin.

NEW DIRECTIONS FOR HIGHER EDUCATION • DOI: 10.1002/he

9

As an alternative to typical top-down mentoring models, the authors advance a conception of peer mentoring that is based on research about collectivist strategies that Latina faculty employ to navigate the academy. The authors advance recommendations for institutional agents to support mentoring for faculty who are members of historically underrepresented groups.

Weaving Authenticity and Legitimacy: Latina Faculty Peer Mentoring

Anne-Marie Núñez, Elizabeth T. Murakami, Leslie D. Gonzales

Faculty women of color face several obstacles to advancement in academia (Núñez & Murakami-Ramalho, 2012; Turner, 2002; Turner, González, & Wood, 2008). Like all faculty women of color, Latina faculty are doubly marginalized due to their ethnicity and gender, meaning that they simultaneously face racism and sexism (Turner, 2002). Because there are often very few Latina faculty members within their departmental setting, Latina faculty also often report isolation, tokenism, and heightened expectations for service to underrepresented groups (e.g., Niemann, 1999; Turner, 2002). Furthermore, Latina faculty have a tenuous presence in academia, particularly among the tenured, senior ranks (Turner, 2011). Latinas compose just 3.4% of all female associate professors and 2.8% of all female full professors in the United States (Chronicle of Higher Education, 2010).

In this piece, we illustrate how a "pedagogy for equity" (Núñez, Murakami Ramalho, & Cuero, 2010) framework provides an approach to mentoring that can facilitate a deeper sense of belonging and legitimacy in academia for women of color. Using this approach entails cultivating recognition of these faculty members as learners, teachers, and, ultimately, knowers. Efforts to support the professional learning and recognition of women faculty of color are of critical importance in light of the extensive evidence regarding the marginalization of women of color as knowers and theorists of their own accord (Collins, 1986; Gutiérrez y Muhs, Niemann, González, & Harris, 2012).

Mentoring from a pedagogy of equity perspective addresses the need to move beyond numerical representation of historically marginalized groups

NEW DIRECTIONS FOR HIGHER EDUCATION, no. 171, Fall 2015 © 2015 Wiley Periodicals, Inc.
Published online in Wiley Online Library (wileyonlinelibrary.com) • DOI: 10.1002/he.20145

in higher education toward making more fundamental changes to higher education organizational cultures and institutional structures (Smith, 2009). Throughout this chapter, we draw from our own previous empirical research and experiences as women of color to discuss how we have applied pedagogy for equity in peer mentoring and in our mentoring relationships with other women/women of color. We then discuss the implications of this work for researchers, developers of mentoring policies or programs, and mentors themselves.

Literature Review

Like many underrepresented individuals and groups within academia, Latina faculty often develop knowledge and theorize about the world in ways that are informed by their personal and cultural experiences (Collins, 1986; Gonzales, Murakami, & Núñez, 2013). For example, Latina faculty are likely to enter the academy with research agendas connected to their communities and are also more likely to study issues related to sexism, racism, and classism in addition to other identity markers (Delgado Bernal & Villalpando, 2002; González & Padilla, 2008; Turner et al., 2008). Accordingly, it is not uncommon for Latina faculty members' approach to knowledge production to challenge traditional and positivist conventions in academic research, which have historically decontextualized and marginalized the experiences of underrepresented people (Stanley, 2007). Thus, Latina faculty may not follow academia's "prescriptions for legitimacy" (Gonzales, 2013, p. 202). These prescriptions are deeply ingrained norms and rules that constrain the valuation of faculty work (Gonzales, 2013).

Many critical scholars agree that these prescriptions privilege scientism, detachment from one's work, and more narrowly focused scholarship (Hart & Metcalfe, 2010). Notably, calls to broaden the definition of scholarship to include community engagement, action-based/applied research, or the scholarship of teaching have had inconsistent success (Boyer, 1990; Jaeger & Thornton, 2006). Consequently, Latina faculty with an orientation to serve their communities may abandon or distance themselves from such orientations in order to conduct work that will be viewed as "legitimate" enough to achieve tenure (González & Padilla, 2008). However, an emerging body of literature shows that faculty members, particularly from underrepresented groups, attempt to negotiate these institutionalized prescriptions by explicitly anchoring their work in specific cultural and historical contexts and experiences that have traditionally been underrepresented in scholarship (Delgado Bernal, 2008; Stanley, 2007; Turner, 2002). With these challenges in mind, it is critical to consider how to encourage, support, and validate such scholars, including Latina faculty, in their efforts to advance in the academy (Gonzales et al., 2013).

Mentoring Toward Legitimacy

Mentoring is often used as a strategy to facilitate the advancement of all women in the academy (Allan, 2011; Ek, Quijada Cerecer, Alanís, & Rodríguez, 2010; Núñez & Murakami-Ramalho, 2012). However, research suggests that women from underrepresented backgrounds (e.g., African Americans, Latinas, Native Americans, those with working-class backgrounds) are less likely to receive mentorship, so it is particularly important to develop intentional mentoring efforts for underrepresented faculty that are validating and inclusive of their perspectives (e.g., Tierney & Bensimon, 1996). Traditionally, conventional mentoring follows a "grooming" model where a junior professor shadows a senior professor (Allan, 2011) to learn how to imitate the mentor. This approach, however, implicitly suggests that "women at lower levels of the organizational hierarchy simply need to 'try harder' and do more of the right things so they too will advance" (Allan, 2011, p. 109). An emphasis on top-down mentoring models that suggest that women faculty of color need to conform to dominant norms in order to be considered "legitimate" and "competent" in the academy can obscure the well-documented institutional obstacles and the responsibility that institutions have to shape conditions for cultivating *all* faculty members' success (Smith, 2009).

Recently, female academics have set up alternative peer mentoring systems to help one another navigate academia (e.g., Allan, 2011; Ek et al., 2010; Gutiérrez y Muhs et al., 2012; Murakami & Núñez, 2014; Núñez & Murakami-Ramalho, 2012). Peer mentoring emphasizes a network approach of sharing resources and presumes that all participants possess distinctive assets to contribute to one another's development. Among women of color, peer mentoring can serve as an opportunity to validate how one's multiple identities shape one's work (Ek et al., 2010; Núñez & Murakami-Ramalho, 2011; Quijada Cerecer, Ek, Alanís, & Murakami-Ramalho, 2011). By challenging hierarchical notions of mentoring and broadening opportunities for those from marginalized groups to support one another, peer mentoring represents an inclusive pedagogy (Tuitt, 2003) for facilitating a sense of belonging and legitimacy in the academy.

Conceptual Framework

Pedagogy for equity is a framework inspired by Mills's (1959) concept of the sociological imagination and informed by Collins's (1990) suggestion that oppression can occur on three levels: (a) personal biography, (b) community or cultural level, and (c) the broader systemic level of institutions. It is defined as an approach to teaching and learning in which faculty and students examine how their personal biographies, sociocultural contexts, and the broader systemic level of social institutions inform research, policy, and practice (Núñez et al., 2010). Here, we extend this approach to inform peer mentoring among faculty. Guiding assumptions include that faculty mentors can serve as teachers and learners, while deconstructing traditional hierarchies of personnel and building inclusive approaches that challenge different types of oppression.

In the context of faculty mentoring, pedagogy of equity practices can be employed at the levels of: (a) personal biography (affirming flexible modes of identity, critically reflecting on assumptions about oneself and others); (b) sociocultural group contexts (understanding one's social identities in relation to one's communities, being responsive to multiple forms of expression, serving as role models); and (c) systemic level of social institutions (challenging traditional notions of educational leadership and mobility, and fostering new ways to enact educational change that is responsive to an increasingly diverse population) (Núñez et al., 2010).

Methods

To consider the application of pedagogy of equity mentoring, we examined mentoring practices and experiences documented in various sources, including: (a) previous articles written by selected faculty (including two of us) who have participated in a collaborative housed within a Hispanic-serving institution (HSI) (Murakami & Núñez, 2014), (b) personal journals of mentoring experiences of Latina faculty from articles and the authors' autoethnographies, and (c) our own dialogues about legitimacy and peer mentoring in academia. As we examined these sources, we asked: How can pedagogy of equity help mentors and mentees foster a sense of belonging and legitimacy for women of color who often challenge the deeply institutionalized "prescriptions for legitimacy" (Gonzales, 2012, 2013) that guide faculty reward systems?

Enacting Pedagogy for Equity Through Peer Mentoring

Connections between the three levels of pedagogy for equity—personal biography, sociocultural group contexts, and the broader systemic level of social institutions—are significant when enacting pedagogy for equity. We identified multiple dimensions of peer mentoring that range from a more individually oriented to a more community-oriented focus. We recognize that some mentoring may straddle multiple levels.

Personal Biography.   On this level, there are opportunities to reflect on exclusionary structures, the pain experienced under these structures, and alternative strengths that may go unrecognized by the dominant culture (Montoya, 2002). For example, girls may often be silenced and not recognized for their ways of knowing (Belenky, Clinchy, Goldberger, & Tarule, 1986), in "school structures [that] tend to ensure that white middle-class students occupy places of privilege, marginalizing working-class and poor students, and students of color" (Vetter, Fairbanks, & Arial, 2011, p. 188).

NEW DIRECTIONS FOR HIGHER EDUCATION • DOI: 10.1002/he

Even early on in elementary education, Latinas experience limited "availability of counter-discourses that acknowledge and validate the knowledge, skills, and other tools [that they] possess" (Vetter et al., 2011, p. 188). By reflecting on early experiences, Latina faculty develop counter-discourses to challenge master narratives prevailing in the academy. Furthermore, through peer mentoring, Latina faculty can articulate long-running experiences regarding their marginalization inside educational institutions, and simultaneously ease feelings of isolation.

In one example, a member of a Latina faculty peer mentoring organization called Research for the Education and Advancement of Latinas (REAL) (Alanís, Cuero, & Rodríguez, 2009) expressed the support she found in this group:

> I think having had the experience of being the only one [Latina] in high school and in junior high and then an undergrad, it's just something amazing to see so many Latinas and Chicanas in one place. . . . I think it's just the feeling of security. . . . I've walked into other spaces where you don't know quite where you belong or where you fit in. (Ek et al., 2010, p. 546)

Reflecting on these personal experiences with members of the group and having a space to express vulnerability in relation to marginalizing experiences allowed this Latina faculty member to find a sense of community and security within her institution.

Because Latinas vary along dimensions like nation of origin, race, ethnicity, and immigration status, reflecting on personal biographies offers peer mentors opportunities to work across identities of difference, fostering a sense of solidarity, or *hermandad* (sisterhood) (Béttez, López, & Machado-Casas, 2008). Thus, Latina faculty see ways they can work together to advance common goals, despite their differences. Through collective reflection, these scholars can cultivate "interest convergence" (Bell, 1980), advancing common research and personal interests that overlap across different social identities (Santamaría & Santamaría, 2012).

Sociocultural Group Contexts.   Through creating collaborative sociocultural group contexts, Latina faculty can build and/or affirm one another's commitment to community. For example, Quijada Cerecer and colleagues (2011) described how Latina faculty who were peer mentors developed *transformative resistance*, or a focus on community advancement in teaching and research. One of the scholars said, "Although the chair of my department suggested I remove myself from the State bilingual organization, I feel that it is my responsibility to advocate for language minority children and bilingual teachers. So, I have chosen to remain a board member" (Quijada Cerecer et al., 2011, p. 84). Collectively affirming one another's commitments to the community is important when such initiatives are "undermined and questioned by mainstream academic culture" (Ek & Rodríguez, 2009, p. 84).

Also at the sociocultural level, Latina faculty can mentor one another by sharing intellectual resources and lenses that may not be typical parts of a curriculum. For example, REAL researchers met to educate one another on different research theories, including critical race theory (Villalpando, 2004), funds of knowledge (Gonzalez et al., 1995), and intersectionality (Crenshaw, 1991). Each of these theories implies that Latina faculty, students, and families hold valuable assets, capital, and knowledge.

Systemic Level of Social Institutions. According to Machado-Casas, Ruiz, and Cantu (2013), academia is a "*laberinto* (labyrinth) [that] contains places that are complicated and uncertain. When you enter a *laberinto* you don't really know the way, or how you will get to the end" (p. 12). Considering the complexity of academia, how can Latina peer mentoring play a role in reshaping a traditional institution such as the academy? One way Latina and other faculty of color can support one another is to share the "hidden curriculum" of academia, including how to build promotion and tenure files (Núñez & Murakami-Ramalho, 2012). Another is by connecting with different disciplinary associations or editorial boards. Additionally, they can advocate the accomplishments of colleagues through their academic communities.

While shadowing a senior Latina is often difficult, due to their limited presence in the academy (Turner et al., 2008; Turner, González, & Wong, 2011), the evidence discussed thus far indicates that Latina faculty and women of color can mentor one another as peers to advance in the promotion and tenure process. Latinas who advance to institutional and national leadership positions can advocate for other Latina faculty and highlight scholarship and academic accomplishments with a reformed "prescription for legitimacy." Such renewed prescriptions could honor the diverse ways of knowing that Latinas (and underrepresented groups, overall) might bring with them to academia, including community-oriented and action-oriented research or culturally sensitive commitments to service and teaching. Peer mentoring is a small step toward challenging the systemic marginalization that Latinas often face in academia.

Implications

Those who develop or evaluate mentoring programs or those who have the ability to support mentoring efforts within academia must provide support that allows for the development of a community of scholars. This means that resources must allow for teaching and learning among the mentors and mentees. Universities must ensure that faculty evaluation practices and policies are crafted and implemented in a way that allows for diversity in knowledge production (Núñez & Murakami-Ramalho, 2012). Specific mentoring practices and supportive policies include the following:

Focus energies around the principle that all individuals are legitimate creators and agents of knowledge (Collins, 1990). Each person's personal, cultural, professional, political, and disciplinary-based backgrounds can be viewed as assets. By building mentoring efforts and relationships around this principle, a traditional hierarchical, compensatory (or deficit), and grooming approach to mentoring is displaced.

Focus conversations and interests into writing projects. These undertakings can generate new lines of inquiry and scholarship. These groups can help scholars be strategic about developing new lines of research that contribute to a coherent agenda as well as a broader community of scholarship.

Teach and learn from one another the practice and value of self-reflexivity. The idea of pedagogy for equity emerged from a group of faculty members' dialogues about their approaches to teaching, the way they relate to their students, and the approach they take toward framing their teaching within broader social contexts (Núñez et al., 2010). Having dialogues about challenges, opportunities, relations of power, and privilege, including the privilege that Latinas have as academics, can help Latina faculty remain cognizant of their motivation for pursuing an academic career and serving in the educational field. This type of reflection is also necessary for conducting community- and equity-oriented scholarship that is authentic and effective.

Foster connections between teaching, research, and service to the community. Absent a solid infrastructure and incentive system to conduct community-oriented research, teaching, and service, peer mentoring can enable faculty to engage more actively in scholarship that addresses community and social problems (Boyer, 1990). For example, the REAL organization presented their research about Latinos in education with members of the local community, in a one-day professional development event for local teachers who received credit for professional development. In this way, peer mentoring allowed these faculty members to share their research with new audiences and to learn from teachers' experiences in the local, largely Latino community (Núñez & Murakami-Ramalho, 2012). Universities must also move toward rewarding such community-oriented work in the tenure and promotion processes (Hurtado & Sharkness, 2008).

In conclusion, we suggest that extending pedagogy for equity to mentoring approaches, especially for underrepresented faculty groups, engenders opportunities to exchange tacit informal and formal knowledge about how to navigate the academy, thereby facilitating a sense of belonging and legitimacy. As we have argued elsewhere (Gonzales et al., 2013), we cannot support prescriptions for legitimacy that have long marginalized women of color, among other underrepresented groups. Accordingly, we see pedagogy for equity mentoring as a way to create distinctive spaces for women faculty of color as they navigate academia and pursue personal and professional commitments to building community, equity, and diverse ways of knowing.

References

Alanís, I., Cuero, K. K., & Rodríguez, M. A. (2009). Research for the educational advancement of Latin@s: A research and professional development collaborative. *NASPA Journal About Women in Higher Education, 2*, 243–244.

Allan, E. (2011). *Women's status in higher education: Equity matters* (ASHE Higher Education Report, Vol. 37, No. 1). Hoboken, NJ: John Wiley & Sons.

Belenky, M. F., Clinchy, B. M., Goldberger, N. R., & Tarule, J. M. (1986). *Women's ways of knowing*. New York, NY: Basic Books.

Bell, D. (1980). *The winding passage: Essays and sociological journeys, 1960–1980*. Cambridge, MA: Abt Books.

Béttez, S., López, J., & Machado-Casas, M. (2008). *When minorities are especially encouraged to apply: Diversity and affirmative action in higher education*. New York, NY: Peter Lang.

Boyer, E. L. (1990). *Scholarship reconsidered: Priorities of the professoriate*. New York, NY: Carnegie Foundation for the Advancement of Teaching.

Chronicle of Higher Education. (2010). Percentage of faculty members by sex, rank, and racial and ethnic group. *Almanac of Higher Education 2010*. Retrieved from http://chronicle.com/section/Almanac-of-Higher-Education/463/

Collins, P. H. (1986). Learning from the outsider within: The sociological significance of Black feminist thought. *Social Problems, 33*(6), S14–S32.

Collins, P. H. (1990). *Black feminist thought: Knowledge, consciousness, and the politics of empowerment*. Boston, MA: Unwin Hyman.

Crenshaw, K. (1991). Mapping the margins: Intersectionality, identity politics, and violence against women of color. *Stanford Law Review, 43*(6), 1241–1299.

Delgado Bernal, D. D. (2008). *La trenza de identidades*: Weaving together my personal, professional, and communal identities. In K. P. González & R. V. Padilla (Eds.), *Doing the public good: Latina/o scholars engage civic participation* (pp. 134–148). Sterling, VA: Stylus.

Delgado Bernal, D. D., & Villalpando, O. (2002). An apartheid of knowledge in academia: The struggle over the "legitimate" knowledge of faculty of color. *Equity and Excellence in Education, 35*(2), 169–180.

Ek, L. D., Quijada Cerecer, P. D., Alanís, I., & Rodríguez, M. (2010). "I don't belong here": Chicanas/Latinas at a Hispanic serving institution creating community through *muxerista*-mentoring. *Equity & Excellence in Education, 43*(4), 539–553.

Ek, L. D., & Rodríguez, M. A. (2009, April). *Divisions that must be crossed: Latina professors' perspectives of hybridity*. Paper presented within the Creating an Interdisciplinary Space of Resistance: (Counter)narratives of a Latina Research Collaborative Symposium at the American Educational Research Association, San Diego, CA.

Gonzales, L. D. (2012). Faculty responses to mission creep: Cosmopolitan views and actions. *Higher Education, 64*(3), 337–353.

Gonzales, L. D. (2013). Faculty sense-making and mission creep: Interrogating institutionalized ways of knowing and doing legitimacy. *Review of Higher Education, 36*(2), 179–209.

Gonzales, L. D., Murakami, E., & Núñez, A.-M. (2013). Latina faculty in the labyrinth: Constructing and contesting legitimacy in Hispanic serving institutions. *Journal of Social Foundations, 27*(102), 65–89.

New Directions for Higher Education • DOI: 10.1002/he

González, K. P., & Padilla, R. V. (Eds.). (2008). *Doing the public good: Latina/o scholars engage civic participation.* Sterling, VA: Stylus.

Gonzalez, N., Moll, L. C., Tenery, M. F., Rivera, A., Rendón, P., & Gonzales, R. (1995). Funds of knowledge for teaching in Latino households. *Urban Education, 29*(4), 443–470.

Gutiérrez y Muhs, G., Niemann, Y. F., González, C. G., & Harris, A. P. (2012). *Presumed incompetent: The intersections of race and class for women in academia.* Boulder, CO: Utah State University Press.

Hart, J., & Metcalfe, A. S. (2010). Whose Web of Knowledge™ is it anyway? Citing feminist research in the field of higher education. *Journal of Higher Education, 81*(2), 140–163.

Hurtado, S., & Sharkness, J. (2008). Scholarship is changing, and so must tenure review. *Academe, 94*(5), 37–40.

Jaeger, A. J., & Thornton, C. H. (2006). Neither honor nor compensation: Faculty and public service. *Educational Policy, 20*(2), 345–366.

Machado-Casas, M., Ruiz, E., & Cantu, N. E. (2013). Women of color faculty *testimonios* and *laberintos*: Validating spaces for women of color faculty in higher education; Introduction to the special issue. *Journal of Social Foundations, 27*(102), 3–16.

Mills, C. W. (1959). *The sociological imagination.* New York, NY: Oxford University Press.

Montoya, M. E. (2002). Celebrating racialized legal narratives. In F. Valdes, J. McCristal Culp, & A. Harris (Eds.), *Crossroads, directions and a new critical race theory* (pp. 243–250). Philadelphia, PA: Temple University Press.

Murakami, E., & Núñez, A.-M. (2014). Latina faculty transcending barriers: Peer mentoring in a Hispanic-serving institution. *Mentoring and Tutoring: Partnership in Learning, 22*(4), 284–301.

Niemann, Y. F. (1999). The making of a token: A case study of stereotype threat, stigma, racism, and tokenism in academe. *Frontiers: A Journal of Women Studies, 20*(1), 111–134.

Núñez, A.-M., & Murakami-Ramalho, E. (2011). Advocacy in the hyphen: Perspectives from junior faculty at a Hispanic-serving institution. In G. Jean-Marie & B. Lloyd-Jones (Eds.), *Women of color in higher education: Turbulent past, promising future* (pp. 171–194). Bingley, UK: Emerald Press.

Núñez, A.-M., & Murakami-Ramalho, E. (2012). The demographic dividend. *Academe, 98*(1), n1.

Núñez, A.-M., Murakami Ramalho, E., & Cuero, K. (2010). Pedagogy for equity: Teaching in a Hispanic-serving institution. *Innovative Higher Education, 35*(3), 177–190.

Quijada Cerecer, P. D., Ek, L., Alanís, I., & Murakami-Ramalho, E. (2011). Transformative resistance as agency: Chicanas/Latinas (re)creating academic spaces. *Journal of the Professoriate, 5*(1), 70–98.

Santamaría, L., & Santamaría, A. (2012). *Applied critical leadership in education: Choosing change.* New York, NY: Routledge.

Smith, D. G. (2009). *Diversity's promise for higher education—Making it work.* Baltimore, MD: John Hopkins University Press.

Stanley, C. (2007). When counter narratives meet master narratives in the journal editorial-review process. *Educational Researcher, 36*(1), 14–24.

Tierney, W. G., & Bensimon, E. M. (1996). *Promotion and tenure: Community and socialization in academe.* New York, NY: SUNY Press.

Tuitt, F. (2003). Afterword: Realizing a more inclusive pedagogy. In A. Howell & F. Tuitt (Eds.), *Race and higher education: Rethinking pedagogy in diverse college classrooms* (pp. 243–268). Cambridge, MA: Harvard Education Publishing Group.

Turner, C. S. V. (2002). Women of color in academe: Living with multiple marginality. *Journal of Higher Education, 73*(1), 74–93.

Turner, C. S. V. (2011). Latinas in higher education: A presence that remains tenuous. Forty years of the program on the status and education of women. *On Campus with Women*, 39(3). Washington, DC: American Association of Colleges and Universities. Retrieved from http://www.aacu.org/ocww/volume39_3/feature.cfm?section=3

Turner, C. S. V., González, J. C., & Wong, K. (2011). Faculty women of color: The critical nexus of race and gender. *Journal of Diversity in Higher Education*, 4(4), 199–211.

Turner, C. S. V., González, J. C., & Wood, J. L. (2008). Faculty of color in academe: What 20 years of literature tells us. *Journal of Diversity in Higher Education*, 1(3), 139–168.

Vetter, A. M., Fairbanks, C., & Arial, M. (2011). "Crazyghettosmart": A case study in Latina identities. *International Journal of Qualitative Studies in Education*, 24(2), 185–207.

Villalpando, O. (2004). Practical considerations of critical race theory and Latino critical theory for Latino college students. In A. M. Ortiz (Ed.), *New Directions for Student Services: No. 105. Addressing the unique needs of Latino American students* (pp. 41–50). San Francisco, CA: Jossey-Bass.

ANNE-MARIE NÚÑEZ *is an associate professor of higher education in the Educational Leadership and Policy Studies Department at The University of Texas at San Antonio.*

ELIZABETH T. MURAKAMI *is a professor and director of programs in educational leadership in the College of Education and Human Development at Texas A&M University–San Antonio.*

LESLIE D. GONZALES *is an assistant professor of higher education in the College of Education at Michigan State University.*

10

This study utilizes a multivocal narrative approach to analyze the dynamics, accomplishments, and challenges of an interdisciplinary doctoral support group consisting primarily of female members. The authors raise issues of power, alliance, troubling expert-novice models of mentoring, and the role of social justice pedagogy in the group.

Enacting Feminist Alliance Principles in a Doctoral Writing Support Group

Beth Blue Swadener, Lacey Peters, Kimberly A. Eversman

"The support group has been an excellent opportunity for me to remain sane in an otherwise very complex web of relationships, commitments, competition, expectations, ambitions, as well as hopes and desires that accompany one's PhD journey." This statement was made by Mikulas, a participant in the dissertation support group, and we argue it is reflective of many doctoral students and early-career scholars. Due to the complex nature of dissertation and scholarly writing, people are seeking out sources of empowerment and building support networks as a way to find success or to break through the constraints within academia. Single (2010) asserts, "Fluent writing does not happen in a vacuum but within a network of supportive writers" (p. 137). She emphasizes the importance of developing a writing routine and argues that having a partner or building collaborative relationships is an effective means to hold oneself accountable. By offering useful tips on "demystifying dissertation writing," Single's work is an example of how young academics are offered advice on how to gain efficacy in the context of the writing and publication process. While advice like this is instrumental, we have observed, as have others (Holley & Caldwell, 2011; Lechuga, 2011; Mullen, 2003; Mullen, Fish, & Hutinger, 2010), that much of the literature on the writing process or mentoring and support groups takes a technical/rational stance, is more oriented at the mechanics of writing, or is focused on the specifics of mentoring models or support groups.

In contrast, this chapter shares and analyzes multiple perspectives on the organization, with the intention of bringing into the foreground voices of writing group participants, and examining the dynamics and impacts of a writing support group for individuals who have completed course work and

NEW DIRECTIONS FOR HIGHER EDUCATION, no. 171, Fall 2015 © 2015 Wiley Periodicals, Inc.
Published online in Wiley Online Library (wileyonlinelibrary.com) • DOI: 10.1002/he.20146

are now completing proposals or writing dissertations. We begin with a brief history of how the group came into being, along with a description of how we are organized, including specific routines and ways in which support is provided, and then provide a brief discussion of relevant literature. This is followed by an overview of major themes identified in the narratives of group members. We conclude with a brief discussion of how group alumni are engaging in similar mentorship with their students, and implications for mentorship.

History of the Group

The group began in spring of 2010 in the wake of a major reorganization, which disestablished a highly ranked, research-intensive College of Education. At the time of this largely unanticipated action, a number of PhD students were reaching candidacy and looking forward to completing their dissertation research in the coming year. As institutional change occurred, graduate students navigating an already unpredictable space and time became increasingly concerned about how the redistribution of faculty members and mentors would influence the dissertation completion process. Working closely with students, the first author proposed a writing support group for advanced doctoral candidates, and the group was formed. Having taught writing for publication several times and mentoring many of the students affected by the reorganization, forming an active peer support group seemed to be an idea whose time had come. While the disestablishment was a catalyst for the formation of the support group, many other people joined because of issues related to problems faced working within other confines of the university, including a desire for more feedback and support.

The initial writing group included students, primarily women, from several majors, including curriculum and instruction, education policy and leadership studies, and justice studies. The number of disciplines and majors grew to include theater, anthropology, public programs, women and gender studies, applied linguistics, and counseling psychology. The group consisted of members with diverse backgrounds. There were students from South Korea, Taiwan, Kenya, Jamaica, the Czech Republic, Turkey, and the United States. Furthermore, the group reflected several forms of intersectionality, and gender, race/ethnicity, sexual orientation, class background, and other markers of identity played a role in the formation and evolution of the group.

The group has kept the same basic structure for its 4 years: namely, meeting every other week, having an active listserv, encouraging participants to have a writing partner or "accountabilibuddy," and sharing various forms of support in a nonhierarchical manner, grounded in feminist ally principles. Meetings consist of a check-in from each person, including where participants are in the writing or data collection process and setting goals for the coming 2 weeks. At times, group members will request additional feedback, e-mailing drafts to other members during the weeks in between. The dynamics of the group reflect the importance of working with nonjudgmental peers or "critical friends," those who are willing to give feedback and edit presentations as well as dissertation chapters. Other roles the group has played include providing feedback on conference presentations and dissertation defense and job talk presentations, and supporting each other in major personal events, including the births of a number of babies to group members. Writing group members also maintained mutual support and friendship through interactions facilitated through an e-mail listserv, and many are Facebook friends. While the listserv allows for important communications to be transmitted regarding meeting times and other logistical aspects of maintaining community, it also has served as a forum for celebrating accomplishments, sharing funding and dissemination resources, and information on dissertation defenses.

Framing the Study

This study was exploratory in nature and is one of the group's first attempts to make sense of how people's participation has influenced the process of being and becoming academics. The findings are descriptive, and as we share the voices and perspectives of participants we address practical realities of dissertation writing and academic work, but also shed light on the significance of learning together and building community. All group members were asked to respond in writing to two prompts: What has the writing group meant to you? How is the group influencing how you see yourself as a mentor? Of more than 40 past and present group members, 11 people shared their reflections and explanations as to how the group is providing or has provided support in the dissertation completion process, in addition to explaining why the group was or is significant to their roles as scholars, graduate mentors, and educators. Written responses to the prompts were sent electronically to this chapter's authors. Each author read the responses first to gain a general understanding of what people were saying, and then we engaged in a more in-depth analysis as a means to identify common topics discussed and to draw out themes in the text.

Emphasizing the collaborative and community-oriented nature of the group, the findings present brief narratives from current and past group members to illustrate dynamics and impacts of the group. While the stories and recollections bring to light the interconnectedness of the group, we acknowledge that there are not discrete themes within our findings, and the influences on people's graduate school experiences and dissertation completion are interrelated, centering on encountering challenges and overcoming them. Thus, in analyzing the data we turned to theories on community of practice (e.g., Wenger, McDermott, & Snyder, 2002) to interpret the structure and dynamics of the group. In addition, we place a particular focus on ways in which democratic practices and feminist ally principles are used to help individuals find their sense(s) of belonging in their academic work. As such, we draw from bell hooks's framework of teaching as a practice of freedom, and use her notions of "homeplace" (1990), "spaces of openness," and "places of possibility" (2003) to give deeper meaning to participants' reflections about being support group members.

Findings: Participant Narratives

The changes that occurred in reorganization affecting the College of Education at the university reflect one way the changing landscape of academic institutions affects the experiences of both students and faculty members, and in turn the relationships or dynamics between mentors and mentees. As the dispersion of faculty occurred, there emerged a desire among students to establish community or find a sense of belonging. Students were seeking out a "homeplace" (hooks, 1990) in which they could find stability, regain trust, and give credence to the collective nature of learning together—in feminist community. It might be obvious to point out that individuals also shared a common endeavor, dissertation completion, and the formation of the group was to ensure that people would accomplish this goal. And while many discussions in the support group focused on the technicalities or logistical aspects of academic research and writing, the type of support the group provided has gone far beyond the basics of dissertation completion. To accomplish holistic and democratic learning experiences, bell hooks (2003) reminds us of the importance of community as well as the presence of hopefulness. Support group member Flora gives credence to the significance of holistic learning. She wrote:

> What this support group embodies and represents to me is a group that genuinely celebrates each member's success, and at the same time provides emotional and moral support, as well as practical advice to students when challenges arise on this convoluted yet exciting road of attaining a PhD.

As many group members were just entering into candidacy, several people felt unsure about the ways in which they could gain the confidence, clarity, and researcher voice needed to move forward. Grace offered the following reflection when she wrote, "Graduate school at [the university] and in particular my program has been quite the emotional challenge. Honestly, I rarely hear the good experience in regard to graduate work. I have felt isolated, inadequate, and lost much of the time." In other cases, individuals would express feelings of uncertainty and describe creative challenges related to dissertation writing. Even with strong support from her mentor, the possibilities of the dissertation were a challenge, as Wen-Ting reflected:

> For me, I felt in the stage of writing the dissertation (and for many doctoral students, it's also the beginning of job search) that life was filled with all

sorts of uncertainty—it has something to do with what sort a person you aspire to be—via the intellectual creation and the imagination and endeavors of pursuing a future you would want to identify yourself with; so the tensions of identities are overwhelming. No clarity can be provided as to how I could accomplish dissertation writing because it is a process of creation, and it takes time to navigate and reflect on what exactly you want to tell the world.

The conversations that transpired during writing group meetings drew out similar reflections of the insecurities people held, including feeling like an "imposter," struggles with the consuming nature of writing, or feeling inadequate with regard to accomplishing life's other responsibilities. Furthermore, it was not unusual for students to speak of their perceived need to comply with stringent guidelines and expectations set by their mentors or committee members. In order to reframe people's doctoral experiences, group members sought to develop an awareness of their competencies and capabilities, emphasizing self-actualization and the formation of a person's healthy self-esteem as a way to exercise or experience freedom (hooks, 2003).

Building and Cultivating Community

According to Wenger et al. (2002), "Communities of practice are groups of people who share a concern, a set of problems, or a passion about a topic, and who deepen their knowledge and expertise in this area by interacting on an ongoing basis" (p. 4). As Mikulas, one of the few males in the group, stated, "This mentoring group is a real community of friends who desire to be active participants in the academic life and remain ever hopeful and encouraging to others as well." Community of practice (CoP) members help each other solve problems and collectively make meaning of the project in which they are engaged. Their bond comes from learning together and knowing colleagues who share similar ideas, problems, and perspectives, and they develop a feeling of a common mission and identity. A newer member of the group, Greg, spoke to this point by discussing the ways in which the meaning of support has changed for him since he began participating in the community. He wrote, "I have used informal networks as 'cheerleaders'; however, they are simply not sufficient to keep a true sense of accountability. I enjoy being able to discuss where I am at with my work and to hear others share similar stories." Flora also reflected:

> I feel that the members have been able to create an environment that is not competitive, rather collaborative, that does not breed envy or jealousy, rather genuine joy in sharing each other's success stories, and that does not pit students against each other as rivals, but rather encourages all of us to collaborate and help create more inclusive communities, schools, and world for all of us to live in.

New Directions for Higher Education • DOI: 10.1002/he

As reflected in Flora's comments, the interactions individuals had with one another helped to break down oppressive structures, whether they were internalized feelings of doubt or discouragement or institutional barriers that inhibited progress. Members of the support group learned, through their engagement in doctoral work and because of personal life experiences, that vulnerability and uncertainty can lead to multiple forms of care and sources of inspiration, empowerment, and liberation—in essence developing and maintaining "spaces of openness" and "places of possibility" (hooks, 2003). Joy commented, "We also rehearse dissertation defenses as a community. We celebrate having a baby, we mourn when one of us lost our loved one. We rejoice when some of us get their work published. It is amazing to have a sense of community." Finding social and emotional support was one of many functions of the group. As Ayfer pointed out, "In addition to its academic support, this group means a social support to me. We always share happiness and sadness of each other."

Breaking Through the Constraints

Support group members and colleagues confronted the challenges they faced by pulling themselves out of isolation and into our network, which in many cases created opportunities for individuals to collaborate with peers across disciplines and also blurred mentor/mentee relationships as each person in the group was considered to be a peer, ally, or "accountabilibuddy." As Mullen and Lick (1999) explain, "feelings of confidence increase for participants who represent themselves; and ... a more integrated professional identity results from synergistic co-mentoring" (quoted in Mullen, 2000, p. 4). Group members accomplished "synergistic co-mentoring" while letting each other know they were not alone in their struggles. As Cynthia reflected, "The number one support this group provided was emotional support. It's sometimes helpful to remember that other people are feeling alone and simply not capable (a fraud!)." Not only did discussions help to challenge negative ideas about oneself, including what can be named as internalized sexism or classism, but participants also learned how to appreciate their skills and knowledge. Additionally, group members learned to improve their self-perceptions through their interactions with one another. A number of strategies intended to flatten, or at least minimize, hierarchies were used to encourage reciprocal mentoring—for example, writing partners. Participants made reference to "intellectual matching" and the fostering of "critical friendships," bringing light to the benefits of camaraderie and collective support. It was not uncommon for some "critical friends" to meet at coffee shops, cafés, and other spaces outside of the university to write, exchange ideas, and encourage one another to stay offline and on track. Wen-Ting acknowledged this point as she wrote that "the request to articulate what you have done and what is the future plan helps prioritize actions (helps with self-regulation). It also lets us focus on plans and actions, instead of uncertain feelings and uneasiness." This is not to say that all members of the group participated using "critical friends" as a source of support. The formation of partnerships and "intellectual matching" was uneven in terms of the consistency and effectiveness of the writing partners, but it contributed to the continuity of the group and likely to the pace of meeting writing deadlines and completing dissertations.

Respecting Individual Diversity and Interdisciplinary Work

The interdisciplinary nature of the group was also considered to be an effective way to challenge assumptions people held about the dissertation completion processes. Whereas the majority of literature on support groups and mentoring in graduate school focuses on people's experiences working within their own disciplines (e.g., the sciences, education, humanities), we discovered that an inherent benefit to the support group was the interdisciplinary structure of the community. As Mikulas put it, "To be able to meet with a group of very friendly and highly motivated students under the leadership of [our mentor] has been refreshing, helped me to set goals and see a broader vision, and allowed me to see the goal of graduation in more complete terms." Ayfer wrote, "We have a diverse group in terms of their majors, research, and culture. This diversity broadens my perspective to my own research and studies." Other members alluded to ways in which the support group served as a mechanism to reduce the stigma associated with certain practices (and sometime people) in academia. People found comfort or confidence in knowing that their peers and colleagues across the university were facing similar challenges and successes as they progressed through their respective programs. Flora observed:

> I value the interdisciplinary and cross-cultural nature of the discussions. I also value that everyone opens up and shares the challenges, doubts, anxieties, and other not-so-light side of their professional experiences, as sometimes just listening to a story and knowing that you are NOT alone can boost morale.

Wenger and his colleagues (2002) have claimed that each member of a CoP has different motivations for belonging, but the main goal is providing a space of support and growth for members. "Some people participate because they care about the focus of the group and want to see it developed. Others are drawn by the value of having a community. … Other members simply want to learn about the practice … what tools work well, what lessons have been learned by master practitioners" (Wenger et al., 2002, p. 44). Kim provides evidence of this as she wrote:

> There were certainly days when listening to others made me feel incredibly inadequate, especially when I was feeling so stuck and alone, but for the most part, the ability to celebrate all the accomplishments of the group helped me recognize and celebrate my own victories.

As the group carries on, the organization and the dynamics are not static, but ever changing. Yet, as it continues, notions of camaraderie and collective support serve as the grounding principles. The group strives to be safe and fluid; there is respect for funds of knowledge and honoring a range of life experiences. Furthermore, as people joined the group, it became evident that responsive approaches to providing support would be necessary. Several group members needed the meetings to be tight, whereby individuals would attend the meetings with the aim of answering specific questions related to their research and writing. An array of writing issues were addressed in meetings and using the listserv as well. These included voice, organization, and ways of writing dissertations that were more like publishable books. We also discussed study designs, methods, and theoretical frameworks, with group members and facilitator sharing an array of resources, from handouts from other classes to book titles and workshop flyers. Reading other group members' drafts and giving critical feedback also played a mentorship role. This exposure to writing across disciplines, styles, and methodologies was helpful background for participants as they prepared to enter higher education careers. Several group members also collaborated with the faculty mentor/facilitator in journal manuscript reviews, and the third author served as editorial assistant for a major education research journal while in the PhD program.

There have been other times when individuals would attend the meetings for knowledge's sake and to hang out with ideas. As Grace reflected, "Having a group of people to bounce ideas off of and to celebrate victories regardless of how big or small has made the experience at [the university] less isolating." Joy adds to this by stating, "The writing group has opened up a lot of possibility to cooperate with colleagues who are going through the same journey."

Conclusion

The group has also discussed paying it forward, or how being part of the writing group was influencing ways in which group members and alumni were mentoring their students or working with colleagues in their field. With 37 group members graduating and obtaining positions primarily in higher education, many have continued to post on the listserv or responded to our questions with examples of ways in which they are mentoring their own students. Some have formed small groups, and others are making manuscript reviewing and coauthoring of manuscripts available to their graduate students. We would like to think our small group is having a ripple effect and is impacting practice and mentoring strategies not only across the United States but also internationally, as several of our alumni have returned to their home countries. Thus, one of the implications that can be drawn from our collective experience is that, while there is a need to focus on the writing process, there is also a great need for holistic, feminist approaches to supporting early-career scholars in their overall socialization to higher education careers. Creating a "homeplace" (hooks, 1990) that included feminist principles such as voice balance and space for critique contributed both to individual members' accomplishments and to group identity.

A metaphor that we have used at times to reflect the ways in which the group functions is like a hammock; we borrow this from earlier writing of Gustavo Esteva, a Mexican activist and founder of the Universidad de la Tierra in Oaxaca, who applied this metaphor to community work in a postdevelopment context. A hammock does not represent a standardized or formulaic approach to mentorship; it adapts to those whom it cradles and represents a changing source of support as it takes different shapes as needed. The group continues to be organically responsive to the needs and funds of knowledge of its changing membership, in a sense providing a hammock for early-career scholars to shape their careers.

References

Holley, K. A., & Caldwell, M. L. (2011). The challenges of designing and implementing a doctoral student mentoring program. *Innovative Higher Education, 37*(3), 243–253.

hooks, b. (1990). *Yearnings: Race, gender and cultural politics.* Boston, MA: South End Press.

hooks, b. (2003). *Teaching community: A pedagogy of hope.* New York, NY: Routledge.

Lechuga, V. M. (2011). Faculty–graduate student mentoring relationships: Mentors' perceived roles and responsibilities. *Higher Education, 62*(6), 757–771.

Mullen, C. (2000). Constructing co-mentoring partnerships: Walkways we must travel. *Theory Into Practice, 39*(1), 4–11.

Mullen, C. (2003). The WIT cohort: A case study of informal doctoral mentoring. *Journal of Further and Higher Education, 27*(4), 411–426.

Mullen, C., Fish, V., & Hutinger, J. (2010). Mentoring doctoral students through scholastic engagement: Adult learning principles in action. *Journal of Further and Higher Education, 34*(2), 179–197.

Mullen, C., & Lick, D. W. (1999). *New directions in mentoring: Creating a culture of synergy.* London, UK: Falmer Press.

Single, P. B. (2010). *Demystifying dissertation writing: A streamlined process from choice of topic to final text.* Sterling, VA: Stylus.

Wenger, E., McDermott, R., & Snyder, W. M. (2002). *Cultivating communities of practice.* Boston, MA: Harvard Business School Press.

BETH BLUE SWADENER *is professor of justice and social inequity and associate director of the School of Social Transformation at Arizona State University in Tempe, Arizona.*

LACEY PETERS *is assistant professor of early childhood education at Hunter College, City University of New York, New York.*

KIMBERLY A. EVERSMAN *is assistant professor of education at Wartburg College in Waverly, Iowa.*

NEW DIRECTIONS FOR HIGHER EDUCATION • DOI: 10.1002/he

INDEX

ORDER FORM SUBSCRIPTION AND SINGLE ISSUES

DISCOUNTED BACK ISSUES:

Use this form to receive 20% off all back issues of *New Directions for Higher Education*.
All single issues priced at **$23.20** (normally $29.00)

TITLE	ISSUE NO.	ISBN

Call 1-800-835-6770 or see mailing instructions below. When calling, mention the promotional code JBNND to receive your discount. For a complete list of issues, please visit www.josseybass.com/go/ndhe

SUBSCRIPTIONS: (1 YEAR, 4 ISSUES)

☐ New Order   ☐ Renewal

U.S.	☐ Individual: $89	☐ Institutional: $335
CANADA/MEXICO	☐ Individual: $89	☐ Institutional: $375
ALL OTHERS	☐ Individual: $113	☐ Institutional: $409

Call 1-800-835-6770 or see mailing and pricing instructions below.
Online subscriptions are available at www.onlinelibrary.wiley.com

ORDER TOTALS:

Issue / Subscription Amount: $ _____

Shipping Amount: $ _____
(for single issues only – subscription prices include shipping)

Total Amount: $ _____

SHIPPING CHARGES:
First Item $6.00
Each Add'l Item $2.00

(No sales tax for U.S. subscriptions. Canadian residents, add GST for subscription orders. Individual rate subscriptions must be paid by personal check or credit card. Individual rate subscriptions may not be resold as library copies.)

BILLING & SHIPPING INFORMATION:

☐ **PAYMENT ENCLOSED:** *(U.S. check or money order only. All payments must be in U.S. dollars.)*

☐ **CREDIT CARD:** ☐ VISA ☐ MC ☐ AMEX

Card number _____ Exp. Date _____

Card Holder Name _____ Card Issue # _____

Signature _____ Day Phone _____

☐ **BILL ME:** *(U.S. institutional orders only. Purchase order required.)*

Purchase order # _____
Federal Tax ID 13559302 • GST 89102-8052

Name _____

Address _____

Phone _____ E-mail _____

Copy or detach page and send to: **John Wiley & Sons, One Montgomery Street, Suite 1000, San Francisco, CA 94104-4594**

Order Form can also be faxed to: **888-481-2665**

PROMO JBNND